ITALIAN
In Your Pocket

NEW
HOLLAND

GLOBETROTTER™

Second edition published in 2012
by New Holland Publishers Ltd
London • Cape Town • Sydney
• Auckland
10 9 8 7 6 5 4 3 2 1

website:
www.newhollandpublishers.com

Garfield House, 86 Edgware Road
London W2 2EA
United Kingdom

Wembley Square, First Floor
Solan Road
Cape Town 8001
South Africa

Unit 1, Gibbes Street
Chatswood, NSW 2067
Australia

218 Lake Road
Northcote, Auckland
New Zealand

ISBN 978 1 78009 426 7

Publishing Manager:
Thea Grobbelaar
Designer: Lellyn Creamer
Cover Design: Nicole Bannister
Illustrator: Marisa Galloway
Editor: Thea Grobbelaar
Translator: Gillian Bugg
Proofreader: Silvana Sabbatino

Reproduction by Resolution, Cape Town
Printed and bound by Times Offset (M)
Sdn. Bhd., Malaysia

Cover photograph: *Alfresco dining in Venice, Italy.*

CONTENTS

PHRASE BOOK

DICTIONARY

This PHRASE BOOK is thematically colour-coded for easy use and is organized according to the situation you're most likely to be in when you need it. The fairly comprehensive DICTIONARY section consists of two parts – English/Italian and Italian/English.

To make speaking Italian easy, we encourage our readers to memorize some general PRONUNCIATION rules (*see* page 8). After you have familiarized yourself with the basic tools of the language and the rudiments of Italian GRAMMAR (*see* page 14), all you need to do is turn to the appropriate section of the phrase book and find the words you need to make yourself understood. If the selection is not exactly what you're looking for, consult the dictionary for other options.

Just to get you started, here are some Italian expressions you might have heard, read or used at some time: *arrivederci*, *ciao*, *presto*, *buon giorno*, *grazie*, *si*, *crescendo*, *amore*. Even if you are unfamiliar with these words and would rather not try to say them out loud, just remain confident, follow our easy advice and practise a little, and you will soon master useful phrases for everyday life. Speak slowly and enunciate carefully and your counterpart is likely to follow suit.

Some Italian words are pronounced a little differently from their English equivalents (e.g. zero – *dzeh-roh*), or else changed just slightly (monument – *monumento*), though their meanings remain clear. Nowadays many English terms are used in Italian, especially in business, sport and leisure activities, so everyone will know what you mean when you say things like 'laptop', 'golf' and 'tennis'.

A section on HOLIDAYS AND FESTIVALS (*see* page 82) provides some background knowledge so that you know what you're celebrating and why. There's no better way to learn a language than joining in some of the enjoyment!

The brief section on manners, mannerisms and ETIQUETTE (*see* page 76) can help you make sense of the people around you. Make an effort to view your host country and its people tolerantly – that way you will be open to the new experience and able to enjoy it.

Learning a new language can be a wonderful but frightening experience. It is not the object of this book to teach you perfect Italian, but rather to equip you with just enough knowledge for a successful holiday or business trip. Luckily you are unlikely to be criticized on your grammatical correctness when merely asking for directions. The most important thing is to make yourself under-stood. To this end a brief section on grammar and a guide to pronunciation have been included in this book. There is, however, no substitute for listening to native speakers.

Before you leave, it might be a good idea to familiarize yourself with the sections on Pronunciation, Grammar and Etiquette. This can easily be done en route to your destina-tion. You will also benefit from memorizing a few important phrases before you go.

The sections of the Phrase Book are arranged by topic for quick reference. Simply go to the contents list (*see* page 3) to find the topic you need. The Dictionary section (*see* page 88) goes both ways, helping you to understand and be understood.

Abbreviations have been used in those instances where one English word could be interpreted as more than one part of speech, e.g. 'smoke' (a noun, the substance coming from a fire) and 'smoke' (a verb, what one would do with a cigarette). Here is a list of these and some other abbreviations used in this book:

vb	verb
n	noun
adj	adjective
adv	adverb
prep	preposition
pol	polite
fam	familiar (informal)
elec	electric/al
med	medical
anat	anatomy
rel	religion

The gender and number of Italian nouns have been specified as follows:

m	masculine
f	feminine
pl	plural

PRONUNCIATION

VOWELS 9
VOCALI 9

CONSONANTS 10
CONSONANTI 10

GENERAL 12
GENERALE 12

Italian is a Romance language which evolved from Latin. The pronunciation of an Italian word is very similar to the way it is written. The stress in Italian usually falls on the second-last syllable (e.g. *casa*, *ragazzo*, *matita*). If the stress is on the last syllable, the Italian word has a written grave accent (e.g. *città*, *verità*).

The Italian alphabet is the same as the English alphabet, but the letters **j**, **k**, **x**, **y** and **w** are found only in foreign words.

VOWELS
VOCALI

The Italian vowels are **a**, **e**, **i**, **o** and **u**. Each vowel has only one sound, but **o** and **e** can be open or closed according to their position:

◆ **a** – pronounced like the **a** in car – *sala (sah-lah)* – hall; but it is shorter in Italian – *la (lah)* – the

◆ **e** – pronounced like the **ai** in s**ai**d – *letto (leht-toh)* – bed; or like the **e** in l**e**mon – *mela (meh-lah)* – apple

◆ **i** – pronounced like the **ee** in m**ee**t – *vino (vee-noh)* – wine

- **o** – pronounced like the **o** in n**o**t – *posta (pos-tah)* – post; or like the **o** in alm**o**st – *sono (soh-noh)* – I am
- **u** – pronounced like the **oo** in m**oo**n – *cura (koo-rah)* – cure

CONSONANTS
CONSONANTI

Most consonants are pronounced the same as in English, with the exception of the following:

- **c** – before **e** and **i**, it is pronounced like the **ch** in **ch**urch – *ci (chee)* – there
- **c** – before **o**, **a** and **u**, it is pronounced like the **k** in **k**ing – *casa (kah-zah)* – house
- **ch** – always pronounced like the **k** in **k**ing – *che (keh)* – that
- **g** – before **e** and **i**, it is pronounced like the **j** in **j**eep – *giro (jee-hroh)* – trip
- **g** – before **o**, **a** and **u**, it is pronounced like the **g** in **g**o – *gara (gah-rah)* – race, *guida (gwee-dah)* – guide
- **gh** – always pronounced like the **g** in **g**ate – *laghi (lah-ghee)* – lakes
- **gli** – pronounced like the **ll** in mi**ll**ion – *luglio (loo-l'yoh)* – July; *gli (l'yee)* – the

- **gn** – pronounced like the **ny** in can**y**on – *ogni (oh-n'yee)* – every
- **h** – not pronounced at all – *ha (ah)* – he has
- **qu** – pronounced like the **qu** in **qu**een – *qui (qwee)* – here
- **r** – rolled like the Scottish **r** – *caro (kah-roh)* – dear
- **s** – it is sharp (like the **s** in **s**ee) before other consonants: *strada (strah-dah)* – road; at the beginning of a word: *sala (sah-lah)* – hall; or when doubled: *sesso (sehs-soh)* – sex
- **s** – between two vowels, it is pronounced like the **z** in **z**ebra – *casa (kah-zah)* – home
- **sc** – before **i** and **e**, it is pronounced like the **sh** in **sh**eet – *sci (shee)* – ski
- **sc** – when followed by a consonant or by an **a**, **o** or **u**, it is pronounced like the **sk** in **sk**y – *scrivo (skree-voh)* – I write; *scusa (skoo-zah)* – sorry
- **z** – at the beginning of a word, it is pronounced like the **ds** in su**ds**y – *zero (dzeh-roh)* – zero
- **z** – elsewhere in a word, it is pronounced like the **ts** in gu**ts**y – *pranzo (prahn-tsoh)* – lunch

GENERAL
GENERALE

When speaking Italian, you should linger on the vowels and not pronounce the consonants too forcefully, except where a consonant has been doubled – e.g. *ditta (deet-tah)*.

Inflection is also important. Remember to make your voice rise at the end of a sentence if it is a question, and to modulate your voice downwards if it is a statement, just as you would when speaking English.

Practise a few phrases in Italian to get the hang of it – stressed syllables are underlined:

Ciao!
chaao
Hello!

Arrivederci!
arreevaydehrchee
Goodbye!

Parla inglese?
parla eengglaysay
Do you speak English?

Non capisco!
Non kapeesko
I don't understand!

Può parlare più lentamente, per favore?
pwo parlaaray peeoo layntamayntay, pehr favoray
Could you please speak more slowly?

Come sta?
komay sta
How are you? (polite)

Come stai?
komay stai
How are you? (familiar)

Bene, grazie!
Baynay graatseeay
Fine, thanks!

Scusi?
skoozee
Pardon?

Per favore!
pehr favoray
Please!

Grazie!
graatseeay
Thank you!

Posso avere ...?
posso avayray
May I have ...?

Vorrei ...
vorrehee
I'd like ...

Ieri
ee-ehree
yesterday

oggi
odjee
today

domani
domaanee
tomorrow

Dov'è la toilette?
doveh la toehlehteh
Where is the toilet?

GRAMMAR

The grammar section has deliberately been kept very brief as this is not a language course.

NOUNS
NOMI

All nouns are either masculine or feminine in **gender**. Masculine nouns usually end in –o, while feminine nouns usually end in –a. Nouns ending in -e can be either masculine or feminine, but their gender can be identified by referring to the definite article ('the') placed before the noun, e.g.

- *il ristorante* – masculine, as *il* is masculine
- *la chiave* – feminine, as *la* is feminine

Some nouns ending in -a refer to both men and women, e.g.

- *l'artista* (m/f) – the artist

To form the **plural** of a noun, all you need to do is change the last letter. Nouns ending in -o and -e will end in -i in their plural form, while those ending in -a will end in -e in their plural form. When changing a noun to the plural form, remember to make the definite article ('the') plural too (see page 18).

ADJECTIVES
AGGETTIVI

Adjectives must agree in **gender** and **number** with the noun they modify. In Italian, the adjective generally follows the noun, e.g.

◆ *un gatto bianco* – a white cat

Sometimes the adjective precedes the noun, for instance when expressing size, e.g.

◆ *una grande casa* – a large house

The **comparative** is formed by placing *piú* (more) or *meno* (less) before the adjective:

◆ large – *grande*; larger – *piú grande*
◆ ugly – *brutto*; less ugly – *meno brutto*

The **superlative** is formed either by placing *il/la/i/le piú* (the most) or *il/la/i/le meno* (the least) before the adjective, or by changing the ending of the adjective to -issimo (if used with a masculine noun) or -issima (if used with a feminine noun), e.g.

◆ very beautiful – *bellissimo, bellissima*

Possessive adjectives, like all adjectives, must agree in gender and number with the

noun they modify, with the exception of
loro (their):

Masculine	Singular	Plural
my	*il mio*	*i miei*
your (fam)	*il tuo*	*i tuoi*
your (pol)	*il Suo*	*i Suoi*
his/hers/its	*il suo*	*i suoi*
our	*il nostro*	*i nostri*
your (pl)	*il vostro*	*i vostri*
their	*il loro*	*i loro*

Feminine	Singular	Plural
my	*la mia*	*le mie*
your (fam)	*la tua*	*le tue*
your (pol)	*la Sua*	*le Sue*
his/hers/its	*la sua*	*le sue*
our	*la nostra*	*le nostre*
your (pl)	*la vostra*	*le vostre*
their	*la loro*	*le loro*

ARTICLES
ARTICOLI

The **indefinite** article ('a' or 'an') is used as
follows:

◆ *un* – before most masculine nouns

- ◆ *uno* – before masculine nouns beginning with **z** or **s** plus a consonant
- ◆ *una* – before most feminine nouns
- ◆ *un'* – before all feminine nouns beginning with a vowel

The **definite** article ('the') is used as follows:

- ◆ *il* – before most masculine singular nouns
- ◆ *i* – before most masculine plural nouns
- ◆ *lo* – before masculine singular nouns beginning with **z** or **s** plus a consonant
- ◆ *gli* – before masculine plural nouns beginning with **z** or **s** plus a consonant
- ◆ *l'* – before masculine singular nouns beginning with a vowel
- ◆ *gli* - before masculine plural nouns beginning with a vowel
- ◆ *la* – before most feminine singular nouns
- ◆ *le* – before most feminine plural nouns
- ◆ *l'* – before feminine singular nouns beginning with a vowel
- ◆ *le* - before feminine plural nouns beginning with a vowel

Since the article varies depending on the inflection (case), the gender of a noun in the dictionary section is only stated as **m** (masculine) or **f** (feminine). A sustained effort is required to memorize all the genders and declensions, but this is not vital in order to make yourself understood.

VERBS
VERBI

There are three types of **regular** verbs in Italian, the infinitive forms of which end in **-are**, **-ere** or **-ire**. To form the **present** tense of these verbs, simply add different endings to the root, e.g. *portare* (to carry):

- port + **o** = *porto* – I carry
- port + **i** = *porti* – you (fam) carry
- port + **a** = *porta* – he/she carries
- port + **iamo** = *portiamo* – we carry
- port + **ate** = *portate* – you (pl) carry
- port + **ano** = *portano* – they carry

The present tense is formed in the same way for verbs ending in **-ere**, but the endings are slightly different: **-o**, **-i**, **-e**, **-iamo**, **-ete** and **-ono**. The endings for verbs ending in **-ire** are **-o**, **-i**, **-e**, **-iamo**, **-ite** and **-ono**.

The **future** tense for verbs ending in **-ere** and **-ire** is formed by removing the final -e and adding **-ò**, **-ai**, **-à**, **-emo**, **-ete** and **-anno**. For verbs ending **-are**, the a changes to e and the same endings are used, e.g. *portare* (to carry): *porterò, porterai, porterà, porteremo, porterete, porteranno*.

To make a verb **negative**, add *non* directly before the verb, e.g.

- *Capisco* – I understand
- *Non capisco* – I don't understand

Familiarize yourself with the present and past tense of some **auxiliary verbs** (for instance 'to be' and 'to have'), which are **irregular** verbs:

Present tense (to be – *essere*)

I am	*io sono*
you (fam) are	*tu sei*
you (pol) are	*Lei è*
he/she is	*lui/lei è*
we are	*noi siamo*
you (pl) are	*voi siete*
they are	*loro sono*

Past tense (to be – *essere*)

I was	*io ero*
you (fam) were	*tu eri*
you (pol) were	*Lei era*
he/she was	*lui/lei era*
we were	*noi eravamo*
you (pl) were	*voi eravate*
they were	*loro erano*

Present tense (to have – *avere*)

I have	io ho
you (fam) have	tu hai
you (pol) have	Lei ha
he/she has	lui/lei ha
we have	noi abbiamo
you (pl) have	voi avete
they have	loro hanno

Past tense (to have – *avere*)

I had	io avevo
you (fam) had	tu avevi
you (pol) had	Lei aveva
he/she had	lui/lei aveva
we had	noi avevamo
you (pl) had	voi avevate
they had	loro avevano

NUMBERS
NUMERI

0	zero *(tzai-ro)*
1	uno *(oo-no)*
2	due *(doo-ay)*
3	tre *(tray)*
4	quattro *(kwatt-ro)*
5	cinque *(cheen-kway)*
6	sei *(say)*
7	sette *(sett-ay)*
8	otto *(ott-o)*
9	nove *(noh-vay)*
10	dieci *(dee-ay-chee)*
11	undici *(oon-dee-chee)*
12	dodici *(doh-dee-chee)*
13	tredici *(tray-dee-chee)*
14	quattordici *(kwa-ttor-dee-chee)*
15	quindici *(kween-dee-chee)*
16	sedici *(say-dee-chee)*
17	diciassette *(dee-cha-se-ttay)*
18	diciotto *(dee-cho-tto)*
19	diciannove *(dee-chan-no-vay)*
20	venti *(ven-tee)*
21	ventuno *(ven-too-no)*
22	ventidue *(ven-tee-doo-ay)*
30	trenta *(tren-ta)*
31	trentuno *(tren-too-no)*
40	quaranta *(kwa-ran-ta)*
50	cinquanta *(cheen-kwan-ta)*
60	sessanta *(se-ssan-ta)*
70	settanta *(se-ttan-ta)*
80	ottanta *(o-ttan-ta)*
90	novanta *(no-van-ta)*
100	cento *(chen-to)*
101	centouno *(chen-too-no)*
120	centoventi *(chen-to-ven-tee)*
500	cinquecento *(cheen-kway-chen-to)*
1000	mille *(mee-lay)*
1 million	un milione *(oon meel-yo-nay)*

DAYS
GIORNI

Monday
lunedì *(loo-ne-dee)*

Tuesday
martedì *(mar-te-dee)*

Wednesday
mercoledì
(mer-ko-le-dee)

Thursday
giovedì *(jo-ve-dee)*

Friday
venerdì *(ve-ner-dee)*

Saturday
sabato *(sa-ba-toh)*

Sunday
domenica *(do-me-nee-ka)*

weekdays
giorni feriali
(jor-nee fe-ree-aa-lee)

weekend
fine settimana
(fee-nay se-ttee-ma-na)

public holidays
giorni festivi
(jor-nee fes-tee-vee)

MONTHS
MESI

January
gennaio *(je-na-yo)*

February
febbraio *(feb-ra-yo)*

March
marzo *(mar-tso)*

April
aprile *(a-pree-le)*

May
maggio *(ma-jo)*

June
giugno *(joon-yo)*

July
luglio *(lool-yo)*

August
agosto *(a-gos-to)*

September
settembre *(se-tem-bre)*

October
ottobre *(o-to-bre)*

November
novembre *(no-vem-bre)*

December
dicembre (*dee-chem-bre*)

TIME
ORA
---

in the morning
di mattina
(*dee ma-ttee-na*)

in the afternoon
di pomeriggio
(*dee po-me-ree-jo*)

in the evening
di sera (*dee seh-ra*)

What is the time?
Che ora è?
(*kay oh-ra eh*)

◆ **it's three o'clock**
◆ sono le tre
  (*soh-no le tre*)

◆ **it's half past two**
◆ sono le due e mezza
  (*soh-no le doo-ay
  eh met-sa*)

◆ **it's quarter to three**
◆ sono le tre meno
  quindici (*soh-no le
  tre meh-no kween-
  dee-chee*)

◆ **twenty past two**
◆ sono le due e venti
  (*soh-no le doo-ay eh
  ven-tee*)

◆ **early**
◆ presto (*pres-toh*)

◆ **late**
◆ tardi (*tar-dee*)

at 10 a.m. (10:00)
alle dieci di mattina
(*allay dee-ay-chee dee
ma-ttee-na*)

at 5 p.m. (17:00)
alle cinque di pomeriggio
(*allay cheen-kway dee
po-me-ree-jo*)

today
oggi (*o-jee*)

tomorrow
domani (*do-ma-nee*)

yesterday
ieri (*yee-ree*)

day after tomorrow
dopodomani
(*do-po-do-ma-nee*)

day before yesterday
l'altro ieri (*lal-troh yee-ree*)

this morning
stamattina
(sta-ma-ttee-na)

yesterday evening
ieri sera *(yee-ree seh-ra)*

tomorrow morning
domani mattina
(do-ma-nee ma-ttee-na)

last night
ieri sera/notte
(yee-ree seh-ra/noh-ttay)

this week
questa settimana
(kwes-ta se-ttee-ma-na)

next week
la settimana prossima
*(la se-ttee-ma-na
pro-ssee-ma)*

now
addesso *(a-deh-sso)*

What is today's date?
Che data è oggi?
(kay da-ta eh o-jee)

It's 20 December
È il venti dicembre *(eh eel
ven-tee dee-chem-bre)*

GREETINGS
SALUTI

Good morning
Buongiorno
(bwon-jor-no)

Good evening
Buonasera
(bwo-na-say-ra)

Good night
Buonanotte
(bwo-na-no-ttay)

Hello/Cheerio
Ciao *(chaa-o)*

Goodbye
Arrivederci
(a-rree-vay-dehr-chee)

See you soon
A presto *(ah pres-toh)*

See you later
A più tardi
(ah pew tar-dee)

Have a good trip
Buon viaggio
(bwon vee-a-jo)

Take care!
Fa attenzione!
(fa a-tten-see-o-ne)

Have a good time
Divertitevi
(dee-_ver_-tee-_te_-vee)

I have to go now
Adesso devo andare
(a-_deh_-sso de-voh an-_daa_-re)

It was very nice
È stato un piacere
(eh _staa_-to _oon_ pee-a-chay-ray)

My name is ...
Mi chiamo ...
(mee kee-_a_-mo ...)

What is your name?
Come ti chiami? (fam)
(_ko_-may tee kee-_a_-mee)
Come si chiama? (pol)
(_ko_-may see kee-_a_-ma)

Pleased to meet you!
Piacere! (_pee_-a-chay-ray)

How are you?
Come sta? (pol.)
(ko-may _stah_)
Come stai? (fam.)
(ko-may _staa_-y)

Just a minute
Un minuto solo
(_oon_ mee-_noo_-to _so_-lo)

	GENERAL GENERALE

Do you speak English?
Parla inglese?
(_paar_-la een-_glay_-say)

I don't understand
Non capisco
(non ka-_pees_-ko)

Please speak very slowly
Può parlare più lentamente, per favore
(pwo paar-_laar_-ay pew len-ta-_mehn_-tay, pehr fa-_vo_-ray)

Please repeat that
Può ripetere, per favore
(pwo _ree_-pe-te-ray, pehr fa-_vo_-ray)

Please write it down
Lo scriva, per favore (loh _skree_-va, pehr fa-vo-ray)

Excuse me please
Mi scusi, per favore (mee _skoo_-see, pehr fa-_vo_-re)

Could you help me?
Mi può aiutare.
(mee pwo a-_yoo_-ta-ray)

Could you do me a favour?
Mi può fare un favore?
(mee pwo <u>faa</u>-re <u>oon</u> fa-<u>vo</u>-ray

Can you show me ...
Può indicarmi ...
(pwo een-<u>dee</u>-char-mee)

how?
come? *(ko-<u>may</u>)*

where?
dove? *(do-<u>veh</u>)*

when?
quando? *(<u>kwan</u>-do)*

who?
chi? *(kee)*

why?
perchè? *(<u>payr</u>-keh)*

which?
quale? *(<u>kwaa</u>-leh)*

I need ...
Ho bisogno ...
(O <u>bee</u>-son-yo)

thank you
grazie *(<u>graat</u>-see-ay)*

yes/no
sì/no *(see/noh)*

FORMS & SIGNS
MODULI E SEGNALI
STRADALI

Please complete in block letters
Completare in lettere maiuscole, per favore
(kom-ple-<u>taa</u>-ray in le-tte-ray ma-yoo-sko-lay, pehr fa-<u>vo</u>-ray)

Surname
Cognome *(kog-<u>no</u>-may)*

First name
Nome di battesimo *(<u>no</u>-may dee ba-<u>ttay</u>-see-mo)*

Date of birth
Data di nascita *(<u>dah</u>-ta dee na-<u>shee</u>-ta)*

Place of birth
Luogo di nascita *(<u>lwo</u>-go dee na-<u>shee</u>-ta)*

Occupation
Mestiere *(mes-<u>tee</u>-ay-ray)*

Nationality
Nazionalità *(nat-<u>see</u>-o-na-lee-ta)*

Address
Indirizzo *(een-<u>dee</u>-ree-tso)*

Passport Number
Numero di passaporto
(*noo-me-ro dee pa-ssa-pohr-to*)

I.D. Number
Numero d'identità (*noo-me-ro dee-den-tee-ta*)

Issued at
Rilasciato a
(*ree-la-shee-at-o ah*)

Date of arrival
Data di arrivo
(*da-ta dee a-rree-vo*)

Date of departure
Data di partenza
(*da-ta dee par-tehn-tsa*)

Engaged, Vacant
Occupato, Libero
(*ok-koo-pa-to, lee-be-ro*)

No trespassing
I trasgressori saranno puniti
(*ee tras-gray-sso-ree sah-ran-no poo-neetee*)

Out of order
Guasto (*gwoo-as-to*)

Don't disturb
Non disturbare
(*non dees-toor-ba-ray*)

Push, Pull
Spingere, Tirare
(*speen-ge-ray, tee-ra-ray*)

Adults and Children
Adulti e Bambini (*a-dool-tee eh bam-bee-nee*)

Lift/Elevator
Ascensore (*a-shen-so-ray*)

Escalator
Scala mobile
(*skaa-la mo-bee-lay*)

Wet paint
Vernice fresca
(*ver-nee-che fres-ka*)

Open, Closed
Aperto, Chiuso
(*a-pehr-to, kee-oo-so*)

Till/Cash Desk
Cassa (*kas-sa*)

Opening hours
Orario di apertura (*o-ra-ree-o dee a-per-too-ra*)

Self-service
Servirsi da soli
(*ser-veer-see da so-lee*)

Waiting Room
Sala d'aspetto
(*saa-la das-peh-tto*)

TRANSPORT

BUS/TRAM STOP
FERMATA DELL'AUTO-
BUS/FERMATA
DEL TRAM

Where is the bus/tram stop?
Dov'è la fermata dell'autobus/del tram?
(*do-veh la fayr-maa-ta dell ow-to-boos/dell tram*)

Which bus do I take?
Quale autobus devo prendere?
(*kwa-lay ow-to-boos day-vo prayn-day-ray*)

How often do the buses go?
Ogni quanto passa l'autobus? (*on-yee kwan-to pah-ssah l'ow-to-boos*)

When is the last bus?
Quando è l'ultimo autobus? (*kwan-do eh lool-tee-mo ow-to-boos*)

Punch your ticket
Validate il biglietto (*va-lee-daa-tay il beel-yay-tto*)

I want to go to ...
Voglio andare a ...
(*vol-yo an-daa-ray ah ...*)

What is the fare to ...?
Quant'è il biglietto per ...?
(*kwan-teh il beel-yay-tto pehr ...*)

Which ticket must I buy?
Quale biglietto devo comperare?
(*kwa-lay beel-yay-tto day-vo kom-pe-raa-ray*)

When is the next bus?
Quando è il prossimo autobus?
(*kwan-do eh il pro-ssee-mo ow-to-boos*)

UNDERGROUND/ SUBWAY/METRO
LA METROPOLITANA

entrance, exit
entrata, uscita (*en-traa-tah, oo-shee-tah*)

Where is the underground station?
Dov'è la stazione della metropolitana?
(*do-veh la stat-sy-o-ne day-lla may-tro-po-lee-taa-na*)

inner zone, outer zone
Zona interna, zona esterna (*tso*-nah in-*tehr*-na, tso-nah es-*tehr*-na)

Do you have a map for the metro?
Avete una carta della metropolitana? (*a-veh-teh oo*-na *kar*-ta day-lla may-tro-po-lee-*taa*-na)

I want to go to ...
Voglio andare a ... (vol-yo an-*daa*-ray ah ...)

Can you give me change?
Puo' darmi il resto? (pwo *daar*-mee il re-*stoh*)

Where must I go?
Dove devo andare? (do-*veh day*-vo an-*daa*-ray)

When is the next train?
Quando è il prossimo treno? (*kwan*-do eh il *pro*-ssee-mo *tray*-no)

How long will it be delayed?
Quanto c'è di ritardo? (*kwan*-to cheh *dee ree*-taar-*do*)

TRAIN/RAILWAY
IL TRENO/
LA FERROVIA

Where is the railway station?
Dov'è la stazione ferroviaria? (do-*veh* la *sta*-tsy-o-ne fe-rro-*vee*-a-*ree*-ah)

departure
partenza (*paar*-ten-sa)

arrival
arrivo (ar-*ree*-vo)

Which platform?
Quale binario? (*kwaa*-le bee-*naa*-ree-o)

a ... ticket please
Un biglietto ... per favore (oon beel-*yay*-tto ... pehr fa-*vo*-ray)

◆ **single**
◆ di sola andata (dee *soh*-lah an-*daa*-ta)

◆ **return**
◆ di andata e ritorno (dee an-*daa*-ta eh ree-*tor*-no)

◆ **child's**
◆ per minorenni (pehr mee-no-*renn*-ee)

- **first class**
- di prima classe
  (*dee pree-ma klass-ay*)

- **second class**
- di seconda classe (*dee say-kon-da klass-ay*)

- **smoking**
- per fumatori
  (*pehr foo-ma-to-ree*)

- **non-smoking**
- per non fumatori (*pehr non foo-ma-to-ree*)

Do I have to pay a supplement?
Devo pagare un supplemento?
(*day-vo pa-gaa-ray oon soo-pleh-men-toh*)

Is my ticket valid on this train?
Il mio biglietto è valido su questo treno? (*il mee-o beel-yay-tto eh va-lee-do soo kwes-to tray-no*)

Where do I have to get off?
Dove devo scendere?
(*do-veh day-vo shayn-day-ray*)

Do you have a timetable?
Avete un orario? (*a-veh-teh oo-na o-ra-ree-o*)

I want to book ...
Voglio prenotare ...
(*vol-yo pre-no-taa-re ...*)

- **a seat**
- un posto (*oon pos-to*)

- **a couchette**
- una cuccetta
  (*oo-na koo-chay-ttay*)

Is this seat free?
È libero questo posto?
(*eh lee-bay-ray kway-sto pos-to*)

That is my seat
Quello è il mio posto (*kwe-llo eh il mee-o pos-to*)

May I open (close) the window?
Posso aprire (chiudere) la finestra? (*pos-so a-pree-ray (kee-oo-de-ray) la fee-nay-stra*)

Where is the restaurant car?
Dov'è la carrozza ristorante? (*do-veh la kaa-rrot-sah rees-to-raan-tay*)

Is there a sleeper?
C'è un vagone letto?
(*Cheh oon va-go-nay leh-ttoh*)

EC – Eurocity
International express, supplement payable

IC – Intercity
Luxury international express, supplement payable

station master
capostazione
(*ka-po-sta-tsy-o-ne*)

BOATS
NAVI

---

cruise
crociera (*kro-chee-rah*)

Can we hire a boat?
Possiamo noleggiare una barca?
(*po-ssee-a-mo no-lay-djaa-ray oo-na baar-ka*)

How much is a round trip?
Quanto costa un biglietto di andata e ritorno?
(*kwan-to kos-ta oon beel-yay-tto dee an-daa-ta eh ree-tor-no*)

one ticket
un biglietto
(*oon beel-yay-tto*)

two tickets
due biglietti
(*doo-ay beel-yay-ttee*)

How long is the trip?
Quanto dura il viaggio?
(*kwan-to doo-ra il vee-a-jee-o*)

Can we eat on board?
Possiamo mangiare a bordo? (*po-ssee-a-mo man-jaa-re ah bohr-do*)

When is the last boat?
Quando è l'ultimo battello? (*kwan-do eh lool-timo ba-tteh-lloh*)

When is the next ferry?
Quando è il prossimo traghetto? (*kwan-do eh il pro-ssee-mo tra-gay-tto*)

Is the sea rough?
Il mare è mosso?
(*il maa-re eh moh-sso*)

I feel seasick
Ho mal di mare
(*o mal dee maa-re*)

TAXI
TASSÌ/TAXI

Please order me a taxi
Mi chiami un tassì, per favore (*mee kee-a-mee oon ta-ssee, pehr fa-vo-ray*)

Where can I get a taxi?
Dove si trovano un tassì? (*do-vay see tro-va-no oon ta-ssee*)

To this address, please
A questo indirizzo, per favore (*ah kwes-to een-dee-ree-tzo, pehr fa-vo-ray*)

How much is it to the centre?
Quanto costa per andare in centro? (*kwan-to kos-ta pehr aan-daa-re in chen-tro*)

To the airport, please
All'aeroporto, per favore (*all-aay-ro-por-to, pehr fa-vo-ray*)

To the station, please
Alla stazione, per favore (*al-la sta-tsee-o-nay, pehr fa-vo-ray*)

Keep the change
Tenga il resto (*ten-gha eel res-toh*)

I need a receipt
Ho bisogno di una ricevuta (*o bee-son-ya dee oo-na ree-ce-voo-ta*)

AIRPORT
AEROPORTO

arrival
arrivo (*a-rree-vo*)

departure
partenza (*paar-ten-sa*)

flight number
numero del volo (*noo-me-ro del vo-lo*)

delay
ritardo (*ree-tardo*)

check-in
accettazione bagagli (*a-chay-tat-see-o-nay ba-gaa-lyee*)

hand luggage
bagaglio a mano *(ba-gaa-lyee-o ah ma-no)*

boarding card
la carta d'imbarco *(la kar-ta deem-bar-ko)*

gate
l'uscita *(loo-shee-ta)*

valid, invalid
valido, non valido *(va-lee-do, non va-lee-do)*

baggage/luggage claim
ritiro bagagli *(ree-tee-ro ba-gaa-lyee)*

lost property office
l'ufficio oggetti smarriti *(loo-ffee-cho oh-jet-tee sma-rree-tee)*

Where do I get a bus to the centre?
Dov'è l'autobus per il centro città? *(do-veh low-to-boos pehr il chen-tro chee-tta)*

Where do I check in for ...?
Dov'è il banco accettazione per ...? *(do-veh eel ban-ko a-chay-tat-see-o-nay pehr ...)*

An aisle/window seat, please
un posto sul corridoio/al finestrino per favore *(oon pos-to sool ko-rree-do-yo/al fee-nes-tree-no, pehr fa-vo-ray)*

Where is the gate for the flight to ...?
Dov'è l'uscita per il volo a ...? *(do-veh loo-shee-ta pehr eel vo-lo ah ...)*

I have nothing to declare
Non ho niente da dichiarare *(non o nyen-tay da dee-kya-ra-ray)*

It's for my own personal use
È per il mio uso personale *(eh pehr eel mee-o oo-so per-so-naa-leh)*

The flight has been cancelled
Il volo è stato cancellato *(eel vo-lo eh staa-to kan-che-llaa-to)*

The flight has been delayed
Il volo è in ritardo *(eel vo-lo eh in ree-tar-do)*

ROAD TRAVEL/ CAR HIRE
VIAGGIARE PER STRADA/NOLEGGIO AUTOMOBILI

Have you got a road map?
Avete una carta stradale? (*a-veh-teh oo-na kar-ta stra-daa-le*)

How many kilometres is it to ...?
Quanti chilometri è lontano ...? (*kwan-tee kee-lo-may-tree eh lon-taa-no ...*)

Where is the nearest garage?
Dov'è l'autorimessa più vicina? (*do-veh low-to-ree-may-ssa pee-oo vee-chee-na*)

Fill it up, please
il pieno, per favore (*eel pee-ay-no, pehr fa-vo-ray*)

Please check the oil, water, battery, tyres
Per favore, controlli l'olio, l'acqua, la batteria, le gomme (*pehr fa-vo-ray, kon-tro-llee lo-lee-o, lak-wa, la ba-tte-ree-a, le gom-meh*)

I'd like to hire a car
Vorrei noleggiare un'automobile (*vo-re-hee no-lay-djaa-ray oon-ow-to-mo-bee-le*)

How much does it cost per week/day?
Quanto costa alla settimana/al giorno? (*kwan-to kos-ta al-la say-ttee-maa-na/al jor-no*)

What do you charge per kilometre?
Quanto costa al chilometro? (*kwan-to kos-ta al kee-lo-may-tro*)

Is the mileage unlimited?
il chilometraggio è senza limite? (*eel kee-lo-may-tra-jo eh sen-sa lee-mee-te*)

Where can I pick up the car?
Dove ritiro l'automobile? (*do-veh ree-tee-ro low-to-mo-bee-le*)

Where can I leave the car?
Dove lascio l'automobile? (*do-veh la-shee-o ow-to-mo-bee-le*)

garage
autorimessa, garage
(*ow-to-<u>ree</u>-<u>may</u>-ssa,
garage*)

headlight
fari dell'automobile (*<u>faa</u>-
ree del-low-to-mo-<u>bee</u>-le*)

windscreen
parabrezza (*pa-ra-<u>bret</u>-sa*)

windscreen wiper
tergicristallo (*ter-<u>gee</u>-
<u>krees</u>-tal-lo*)

What is the speed limit?
Quanto è il limite della
velocita? (*<u>kwan</u>-to eh ee
<u>lee</u>-<u>mee</u>-te day-la ve-lo-
<u>chee</u>-ta*)

The keys are locked in the car
Le chiavi sono chiuse
nella macchina (*le kee-
<u>aa</u>-<u>vee</u> <u>so</u>-no kee-<u>oo</u>-se
nel-la ma-<u>kkee</u>-na*)

The engine is overheating
Il motore è troppo caldo
(*eel mo-<u>to</u>-reh eh <u>trop</u>-
poh <u>kal</u>-do*)

Have you got ...
Avete ...? (*a-<u>veh</u>-teh ...*)

◆ **a towing rope**
◆ un cavo per rimorchiare
(*oon <u>ka</u>-vo pehr
<u>ree</u>-mor-<u>kee</u>-<u>a</u>-ray*)

◆ **a screwdriver/ spanner**
◆ un cacciavite/una chiave
inglese (*oon ka-<u>chee</u>-a-
<u>vee</u>-te/<u>oo</u>-na kee-<u>aa</u>-
vee een-<u>glay</u>-say*)

> **SIGNS**
> SEGNALI STRADALI

No through road
Divieto di transito (*dee-
<u>veeh</u>-to dee tran-<u>see</u>-to*)

one-way street
senso unico
(*<u>sen</u>-so <u>oo</u>-ni-ko*)

entrance
entrata (*en-<u>traa</u>-tah*)

exit
uscita (*oo-<u>shee</u>-tah*)

Keep entrance clear
Passo carrabile (*<u>pa</u>-sso
ka-rra-<u>bee</u>-le*)

Residents only
Solo residenti
(*<u>so</u>-lo re-see-<u>den</u>-tee*)

pedestrians
pedoni (pe-do-_nee_)

danger
pericolo (pe- _ree_-co-lo)

speed limit
Il limite di velocità (eel _lee_-_mee_-te dee ve-lo-_chee_-ta)

No entry
Divieto di accesso (dee-_vee_-hto dee a-_che_-sso)

roundabout
Rotonda (roh-_ton_-da)

Toll
Pedaggio (pe-da-_jee_-o)

Insert coins
Inserire monete (een-se-_ree_-ray mo-ne-_teh_)

Returned coins
Monete di resto
(mo-ne-_teh_ dee _res_-toh)

No parking
Sosta vietata
(sos-tah _vee_-_ay_-ta-ta)

paying car park
parcheggio a pagamento
(par-_kay_-djo ah pa-ja-_men_-toh

unattended car park
parcheggio incustidito
(par-_kay_-djo in-_coo_-sto-_dee_-to)

No right turn
Svolta a destra proibita
(_svol_-ta ah _day_-stra pro-ee-_bee_-ta)

cul de sac
vicolo cieco
(_vee_-ko-lo _chee_-ay-ko)

detour
deviazione (de-_vee_-at-see-_o_-ne)

No admission for un-
authorized persons
Vietato l'accesso ai non
autorizzati (_vee_-_ay_-ta-to la-_chess_-o ay non ow-to-ree-_tsaa_-tee)

Caution
Attenzione
(a-tten-see-_o_-nay)

No stopping
Sosta vietata
(sos-tah _vee_-ay-ta-ta)

No overtaking
Vietato il sorpasso
(_vee_-_ay_-ta-to eel sor-_paa_-ssoh)

ACCOMMODATION
ALLOGGIO

hotel
albergo *(al-bayr-go)*

bed & breakfast
camera e prima
colazione *(ka-may-ra eh
pree-ma ko-la-tsyo-ne)*

vacancies
camere libere *(ka-may-
reh lee-be-ray)*

Have you a room ...?
Avete una camera ...?
*(a-ve-teh oo-na
ka-may-ra ...)*

- ◆ **for tonight**
- ◆ per stanotte
  (pehr sta-noh-tte)

- ◆ **with breakfast**
- ◆ con prima colazione
  *(kon pree-ma
  ko-la-tsy-o-ne)*

- ◆ **with bath**
- ◆ con bagno
  (kon ban-yo)

- ◆ **with shower**
- ◆ con doccia
  (kon dot-cha)

- ◆ **single room**
- ◆ camera singola
  (ka-may-ra seen-go-la)

- ◆ **double room**
- ◆ camera doppia
  (ka-may-ra do-ppee-a)

- ◆ **family room**
- ◆ camera per famiglia
  *(ka-may-ra pehr
  fa-mee-lya)*

**How much is the
room ...?**
Quanto costa la
camera ...? *(kwan-to
kos-ta la ka-may-ra)*

- ◆ **per day/week**
- ◆ al giorno/alla settimana
  *(al jor-no/al-la set-tee-
  maa-na)*

**Have you got
anything cheaper/
better?**
Ne avete un'altra che
costa meno/migliore?
*(neh a-ve-teh oon-al-trah
kay kos-ta me-noh/mee-
lee-o-reh)*

May I see the room?
Posso vedere la camera?
*(pos-so ve-de-ray la ka-
may-ra)*

Do you have a cot?
Avete un lettino? *(a-ve-teh oon le-ttee-noh)*

What time is breakfast/dinner?
A che ora è la prima colazione/il pranzo? *(a kay o-rah eh la pree-ma ko-la-tsy-o-ne/ eel prant-so)*

room service
servizio in camera *(sayr-vee-tsee-o in ka-may-ra)*

Please bring ...
Per favore portatemi ... *(pehr fa-vo-ray por-ta-te-mee)*

♦ **toilet paper**
♦ la carta igienica *(la kar-ta ee-jee-nee-ka)*

♦ **clean towels**
♦ degli asciugamani puliti *(day-lee a-shoo-ga-maa-nee poo-lee-tee)*

Please clean ...
Per favore pulite ... *(pehr fa-vo-ray poo-lee-te)*

♦ **the bath/washbasin**
♦ il bagno/lavandino *(eel baan-yo/la-van-dee-no)*

Please put fresh sheets on the bed
Per favore cambiate le lenzuola *(pehr fa-vo-ray kam-bee-at-ay leh len-tswo-la)*

Please don't touch ...
Vi prego di non toccare ... *(vee pre-goh dee non to-kaa-reh)*

♦ **my briefcase**
♦ la mia borsa
 (la mee-a bor-sah)

♦ **my laptop**
♦ il mio laptop
 (eel mee-o laptop)

My ... doesn't work
La ... non funziona *(la... non foon-see-o-na*

♦ **toilet**
♦ toilette
 (toy-let-te)

♦ **bedside lamp**
♦ lampada da letto
 (lam-pa-dah da leh-tto)

There is no hot water
Non c'è aqua calda *(non che ak-wa kal-da)*

RECEPTION
RICEVIMENTO

Are there any messages for me?
Ci sono dei messaggi per me? (_chee_ _so_-no day me-_ssa_-jee)

Has anyone asked for me?
Mi ha cercato qualcuno? (_mee_ a _cher_-ka-to kwal-_koo_-no)

Can I leave a message for someone?
Posso lasciare un messaggio per qualcuno? (_pos_-so la-_shee_-a-ray oon mess-_a_-jee-o pehr kwal-_koo_-no)

Is there a laundry service?
Avete un servizio lavanderia? (a-ve-teh oon ser-_veet_-see-o la-van-de-_ree_-a)

I need a wake-up call at 7 o'clock
Debbo essere svegliato alle sette (deb-_boh_ e-_sseh_-reh sve-_llee_-a-to all-eh _seh_-tteh)

What number must I dial for room service?
Che numero debbo fare per servizio in camera? (kay _noo_-me-ro deb-_boh_ _faa_-ray pehr ser-_veet_-see-o in _ka_-may-ra)

Where is the lift/elevator?
Dov'è l'ascensore? (do-_veh_ la-shayn-_so_-ray)

Do you arrange tours?
Organizzate gite turistiche? (or-ga-nee-_zaa_-tay jee-teh too-_ree_-stee-ke)

Please prepare the bill
Preparate il conto per favore (pre-pa-_raa_-tay eel _kon_-to pehr fa-_vo_-ray)

There is a mistake in the bill
C'è un errore nel conto (che oon ay-_rro_-ray nel _kon_-to)

I'm leaving tomorrow
Parto domani (_paar_-to do-_ma_-nee)

SELF-CATERING
ALLOGGIO
SELF-SERVICE

Have you any vacancies?
Avete camere libere?
(a-ve-_teh_ _ka_-may-ra _lee_-be-ray)

How much is it per night/week?
Quanto costa alla notte/settimana? (_kwan_-to _kos_-ta _al_-lah _noh_-tte/_se_-ttee-_maa_-na)

How big is it?
Com'è grande?
(_ko_-may _graan_-day)

Do you allow children?
È permesso alloggiare bambini? (eh pehr-_mess_-o allo-_jee_-a-ray bam-_bee_-nee)

Please, show me how ... works
Per favore mi faccia vedere come funziona ...
(pehr _fa_-vo-ray mee _fa_-cha _ve_-de-ray _ko_-may _foon_-see-o-na)

the cooker/stove, the oven
- la stufa, il forno
  (la _stoo_-fa, eel _for_-noh)

the washing machine
- la lavatrice
  (la la-va-_tree_-che)

the dryer
- l'asciugatrice (la-_shee_-oo-ga-tree-che)

the hair-dryer
- l'asciugacapelli (la-_shee_-oo-ga-ka-_pel_-lee)

the heater
- il riscaldamento (_eel_ rees-kal-da-_men_-toh)

the water heater
- il bollitore per l'acqua
  (eel bo-_llee_-to-reh pehr _lak_-wa)

Where is/are ...?
Dov'è/dove sono ...?
(do-_veh_ _so_-no)

the switch
- l'interruttore
  (leen-te-_rroo_-tto-re)

the fuses
- I fusibili (ee foo-_see_-bee-lee)

Is there ...?
C'è ...? *(che)*

- **a cot**
- un lettino *(oon let-<u>tee</u>-no)*

- **a high chair**
- un seggiolone
  (oon se-<u>jee</u>-o-lo-neh)

- **a safe**
- una cassaforte
  (<u>oo</u>-na <u>kas</u>-sa-for-teh)

We need more ...
Ci servono più ...
(chee ser-von-<u>oh</u> pew ...)

- **cutlery**
- coltelleria *(<u>kol</u>-telle-ree-a)*

- **crockery**
- stoviglie *(sto-<u>veel</u>-yay)*

- **sheets**
- lenzuola *(lent-<u>swo</u>-la)*

- **blankets**
- coperte *(<u>ko</u>-per-teh)*

- **pillows**
- cuscini *(<u>koo</u>-shee-nee)*

Is there ... in the vicinity?
C'è ... qui vicino? *(che ... kwee vee-<u>cee</u>-no)*

- **a shop**
- un negozio
  (oon ne-<u>gots</u>-yo)

- **a restaurant**
- un ristorante
  (oon rees-to-<u>ran</u>-te)

- **a bus/tram**
- un autobus/un tram
  (oon <u>ow</u>-to-boos/oon tram)

We would like to stay for ...
Vorremmo stare ...
(vor-<u>rehm</u>-mo <u>sta</u>-ray ...)

- **three nights**
- tre notti *(tre <u>not</u>-tee)*

- **one week**
- una settimana
  (<u>oo</u>-na se-tee-<u>maa</u>-na)

I have locked myself out
Mi sono chiuso fuori *(mee <u>so</u>-no kee-<u>oo</u>-so <u>fwo</u>-ree)*

The window won't open/close
La finestra non si apre/chiude
(la fee-<u>nes</u>-trah non see a-pray/kee-<u>oo</u>-deh)

CAMPING
CAMPEGGIO

caravan
carovana *(ka-ro-va-na)*

Have you got a list of camp sites?
Avete una lista dei campeggi? *(a-ve-teh oo-na lees-ta day kam-pe-jee)*

Are there any sites available?
Ci sono dei posti liberi? *(chee so-no day pos-tee lee-be-ree)*

How much is it per night/week?
Quanto costa alla notte/settimana? *(kwan-to kos-ta al-la noh-tte/ set-tee-maa-na)*

Can we park the caravan here?
Possiamo parcheggiare qui? *(pos-see-a-mo par-ke-jaa-ray kwee)*

Can we camp here overnight?
Possiamo pernottare qui? *(pos-see-a-mo per-noh-tta-ray kwee)*

This site is very muddy
Questo posto è pieno di fango *(kwes-to poh-sto eh pee-ay-no dee fan-goh)*

Is there a sheltered site?
Non c'è un posto più riparato?
(non che oon poh-sto pew ree-pa-ra-toh)

Do you have electricity?
Avete l'elettricità? *(a-ve-teh le-lett-ree-chee-ta)*

Is there ... in the vicinity
C'è nei dintorni ...?
(che nay deen-tor-nee)

◆ **a shop**
◆ un negozio
  (oon ne-gots-yo

◆ **un restaurant**
◆ un ristorante
  (oon rees-to-ran-te)

◆ **an eating place**
◆ uno spaccio alimentari
  (oo-no spa-cho a-lee-men-ta-ree)

- **a garage**
- un autorimessa *(oon ow-to-ree-mes-sa)*

We would like to stay for ...
Vorremmo stare ... *(vo-rreh-mmo staa-ray)*

- **three nights**
- tre notti *(tre not-tee)*

- **one week**
- una settimana *(oo-na se-ttee-maa-na)*

Is there drinking water?
C'è acqua potabile? *(che ak-wa po-ta-bee-leh)*

Can I light a fire here?
Posso fare un fuoco qui? *(pos-so faa-ray oon fwo-ko kwee)*

I'd like to buy fire wood
Vorrei comprare della legna *(vor-ray kom-pra-ray del-la len-ya)*

Is the wood dry?
La legna è asciutta? *(la len-ya eh a-shee-oo-tta)*

Do you have ... for rent?
Avete ... da affittare? *(a-ve-teh ... da a-ffee-ta-ray)*

- **a tent**
- una tenda *(oo-na ten-da)*

- **a gas cylinder**
- una bombola di gas *(oo-na bom-bo-lah dee gas)*

- **a groundsheet**
- un telone impermeabile *(oon te-lo-neh eem-per-me-a-bee-lay)*

- **cooking utensils**
- degli utensili di cucina *(day-lee oo-ten-see-lee dee ku-chee-na)*

Where is the nearest ...?
Dov'è i/la/il ... più vicino? *(do-veh ee/la/eel ...pew vee-cee-no)*

- **toilet block**
- gabinetti *(ga-bee-net-tee)*

- **sink (for washing dishes)**
- secchiaio *(se-kee-ay-o)*

CUTLERY
POSATE

knife
coltello (_kol_-tell-oh)

fork, cake fork
forchetta, forchetta da
torta (for-_ke_-ttah, for-_ke_-
ttah dah _tor_-tah)

spoon, teaspoon
cucchiaio, cucchiaino
(_koo_-kya-yo, koo-kya-
ee-no)

crockery
stoviglie (sto-_veel_-yay)

plate
piatto (pee-_att_-oh)

cup and saucer, mug
tazza e piattino. boccale
(_tat_-sah eh pee-a-_tee_-
noh, bo-_kaa_-leh)

BREAKFAST
PRIMA COLAZIONE

coffee
caffè (kaf-_fay_)

◆ **black**
◆ nero (_nai_-roh)

◆ **with milk, cream**
◆ con latte, panna per il
   caffè (kon _lat_-tay, _pah_-
   nnah pehr eel kaf-_fay_)

◆ **without sugar**
◆ senza zucchero
   (_sen_-tsa _tzoo_-kai-roh)

tea
tè (tay)

◆ **with milk, lemon**
◆ con latte, limone
   (kon _lat_-tay, _lee_-mo-_nay_)

bread
pane (_paa_-nay)

rolls
panini (paa-_nee_-nee)

egg(s) ...
uovo/uova ...
(_wo_-vo/_wo_-va ...)

◆ **boiled – soft, hard**
◆ bollito – alla coque,
   sodo (bo-_lee_-to – _al_-lah
   kok-way, _soh_-doh)

◆ **fried**
◆ fritte (_free_-ttay)

◆ **scrambled**
◆ strapazzate
   (stra-patt-_saa_-tay)

- **poached**
- in camicia
  (in ka-mee-cha)

bacon and eggs
pancetta e uova
(pan-chet-ta eh wo-va)

cereal
cereali *(che-re-al-ee)*

hot milk, cold milk
latte caldo, latte freddo
*(lat-tay kal-do, lat-tay
fred-doh)*

fruit
frutta *(froo-tta)*

orange juice
succo d'arancia
(zoo-koh da-ran-chay)

jam
marmellata
(mar-may-llaa-ta)

marmalade
marmellata d'arance
*(mar-may-llaa-ta da-
ran-chay)*

pepper
pepe *(peh-peh)*

salt
sale *(saa-leh)*

LUNCH/DINNER
IL PRANZO/LA CENA

**Could we have a
table ...?**
Possiamo avere una
tavola ...? *(pos-see-aa-
mo a-vay-ray oo-na ta-
voh-lah ...)*

- **outside**
- fuori *(fwo-ree)*

- **inside**
- dentro *(den-troh)*

May I have ... ?
Posso avere ... ?
(pos-so a-vay-ray ...)

- **the menu**
- il menù *(eel me-noo)*

- **the wine list**
- la lista dei vini
  (la lees-ta day vee-nee)

- **the menu of the day**
- il menù del giorno *(eel
  me-noo del jor-no)*

- **the snack list**
- la lista degli spuntini
  *(la lees-ta day-lee
  spoon-tee-nee)*

◆ **starters**
◆ gli antipasti
(lyee an-tee-pas-tee)

◆ **main course**
◆ la portata principale
(la por-taa-ta preen-chee-paa-le)

◆ **dessert**
◆ il dolce *(eel dol-chay)*

I'll take the set menu
Scelgo il menù fisso
(skayl-goh eel me-noo fee-sso)

What is this?
Che cos' è questo?
(kay ko-zay eh kwes-to)

That is not what I ordered
Non ho ordinato questo
(non o or-dee-naa-to kwes-to)

It's tough, cold, off
È duro, freddo, avariato
(eh doo-ro, freh-ddo, a-va-ree-a-to)

What do you recommend?
Che cosa raccomanda?
(kay ko-za ra-ko-maan-da)

Can I have the bill please?
Il conto per favore? *(eel kon-to pehr fa-vo-ray)*

We'd like to pay separately
Vorremmo pagare separatamente *(vo-rreh-mmo pa-gaa-ray say-pa-ra-ta-mayn-tay)*

There is a mistake
C'è un errore
(che oon eh-rro-ray)

Thank you, that's for you
Grazie, questo è per voi
(graat-see-ay, kwes-to eh pehr voy)

Keep the change
Tenga il resto
(tayn-ga eel reh-sto)

DRINKS
BEVANDE

a beer/lager large, small
una birra
grande, piccola
(oo-na beer-ra gran-day, pee-ko-la)

51

EATING AND DRINKING

half a liter
mezzo litro
(_met_-so _lee_-tro)

amaro (bitter liqueur)
amaro (a-_maa_-roh)

grappa (grape spirits)
grappa (_grah_-pa)

maraschino
maraschino
(ma-ras-_kee_-no)

a dry white wine
un vino bianco secco
(oon _vee_-no bee-_an_-ko _sek_-ko)

a sweet white wine
un vino bianco dolce
(_oon_ _vee_-no bee-_an_-ko _dol_-chay)

a light red wine
un vino rosso leggero
(_oon_ _vee_-no _roh_-sso _lay_-je-roh)

a full-bodied red wine
un vino rosso robusto
(_oon_ _vee_-no _roh_-sso ro-_boos_-to)

a bottle
una bottiglia
(_oo_-na bo-_tteel_-ya)

a glass
un bicchiere (oon beek-_yai_-ray)

sparkling wine
spumante
(spoo-_man_-tay)

house wine
vino di casa
(_vee_-no dee _ka_-za)

brandy
cognac (_kon_-yak)

whisky with ice
whisky con ghiaccio
(whisky kon gee-_a_-cho)

whisky without ice
whisky senza ghiaccio
(whisky _sen_-sa _gee_-a-cho)

mineral water – still, sparkling
acqua minerale – naturale, frizzante (_ak_-wa mee-nay-_raa_-lay – na-too-_raa_-lay, freet-_san_-tay)

tap water
acqua normale
(_ak_-wa nor-_maa_-lay)

fruit juice
succo di frutta
(_zoo_-koh dee _froo_-tta)

52

tomato juice
succo di pomodoro
(_zoo_-koh dee po-moh-_doh_-roh)

liqueur
liquore (lee-_kwo_-ray)

another ... please
un'altro ... per favore (oon-_al_-troh ... pehr fa-_vo_-ray)

too cold
troppo freddo
(_trop_-po _freh_-ddo)

not cold enough
non è freddo abbastanza
(non eh _freh_-ddo abba-_stant_-sa)

FOOD
CIBO

SOUP
MINESTRA (mee-_nes_-tra)

potato soup, mushroom soup
minestra di patate, funghi
(mee-_nes_-tra dee pa-_ta_-tay, _foon_-gee)

celery and rice soup
minestra di sedano e riso
(mee-_nes_-tra dee say-_da_-no eh _ree_-so)

pea, bean, lentil soup
minestra di piselli, fagioli, lenticchie (mee-_nes_-tra dee pee-_sell_-ee, fa-_jo_-lee, len-_teek_-yay)

noodle soup
minestra con pastina
(mee-_nes_-tra kon pas-_tee_-na)

thick vegetable soup with noodles
minestrone
(_mee_-nes-_tro_-nay)

FISH
PESCE (_pe_-shay)

sole
sogliola (_sol_-yo-la)

mackerel
sgombro (sghom-broh)

cuttlefish
seppia (_sep_-pee-a)

cod
merluzzo (mair-_loo_-tzo)

salmon
salmone (sal-_mo_-nay)

herring
arringa (a-_reen_-ga)

trout
trota (*troh*-ta)

turbot
rombo (*rohm*-bo)

tuna
tonno (*tohn*-no)

fried, grilled, sautéed
fritto, alla griglia, saltato
(*free*-tto, al-lah *greel*-ya,
sal-*taa*-to)

POULTRY
POLLAME (pol-*la*-may)

chicken
pollo (*pohl*-lo)

stuffed roast chicken
pollo arrosto ripieno
(*pohl*-lo ar-*ros*-to reep-
yay-no)

duck
anatra (*aa*-na-tra)

goose
oca (*o*-ka)

roasted, fried, grilled
arrosto, fritto, alla griglia
(ar-*ros*-to, *free*-tto, *al*-lah
greel-ya)

MEAT
CARNE (*kar*-nay)

veal
vitello (vee-*tehl*-lo)

mutton, lamb
montone, agnello
(mon-to-nay, an-*yeh*-llo)

beef
manzo (*mand*-zo)

pork
maiale (ma-ee-*aa*-lay)

sausage
salsiccia (sal-*seet*-chay)

venison
carne di cervo
(*kar*-nay dee cher-*voh*)

cured ham
prosciutto crudo (pro-
shoot-to *kroo*-do)

smoked ham
prosciutto affumicato
(pro-*shoot*-to
a-ffoo-mee-*kaa*-to)

meat balls/cakes
polpette (pol-*pet*-tay)

**well-done, medium,
rare**
ben cotto, a mezza
cottura, al sangue
(*behn* *kot*-to, ah *met*-za
kot-*too*-ra, al *san*-way)

boiled, stewed
bollito, in umido (boll-_ee_-to, in _oo_-mee-do)

beef stew
stracotto (di manzo) (stra-_kot_-to [dee _mand_-zo])

brawn
soppressata
(sop-preh-_ssaa_-ta)

platter of cold meats
piatto da portata di affettati
(pee-_atto_ da por-_taa_-ta dee a-ffeh-_ttaa_-tee)

salami
salame (sa-_laa_-may)

pork – smoked
maiale affumicato
(ma-ee-_aa_-lay a-ffoo-mee-_kaa_-to)

bacon – smoked
pancetta affumicata
(pan-_chet_-ta a-ffoo-mee-_kaa_-to)

rice with peas
risotto con piselli (ree-_sot_-to kon pee-_sel_-lee)

dumplings with polenta
suricitti
(soo-ree-_cheet_-tee)

dumplings with cheese and egg
strangolapreti
(stran-go-la-_pray_-tee)

pasta made with cottage cheese
pasta con ricotta
(_pas_-ta kon ree-_kot_-ta)

pasta and chick peas
pasta e ceci
(_pas_-ta eh _chay_-chee)

VEGETABLES, SALAD AND FRUIT
VERDURE, INSALATA E FRUTTA (vair-_doo_-ray, een-sa-_laa_-ta eh _froo_-tta)

green cabbage
verza (_ver_-tza)

cabbage
cavolo (_ka_-voh-lo)

cauliflower
cavolfiore (ka-vol-_fyo_-ray)

carrots
carote (ka-_ro_-tay)

leek
porro (_pohr_-ro)

asparagus
asparagi (as-_pa_-ra-jee)

mushrooms
funghi (*foon*-gee)

peppers
peperoni (pe-pe-*ro*-nee)

pumpkin
zucca (*tzoo*-ka)

potatoes – boiled, fried, mashed
patate – bollite, fritte, purè (pa-*tah*-tay – boh-*lee*-tay, *free*-tay, *poo*-ray)

lettuce
lattuga (la-*ttoo*-ga)

beetroot
barbabietola (bar-ba-*bya*-to-la)

cucumber
cetriolo (che-tree-*o*-lo)

tomato
pomodoro (po-moh-*doh*-ro)

root celery
sedano (say-*da*-no)

green beans
fagiolini (fa-jo-*lee*-nee)

apples
mele (*may*-lay)

pears
pere (*pair*-ay)

bananas
banane (ba-*naa*-nay)

pineapple
ananas (*aa*-na-nas)

apricots
albicocche (al-bee-*ko*-chay)

peaches
pesche (*pes*-kay)

blueberries
mirtilli (meer-tee-llee)

strawberries
fragole (*fraa*-go-lay)

raspberries
lamponi (lam-*po*-nee)

redcurrants
ribes (*ree*-bes)

blackcurrants
ribes nero (*ree*-bes *neh*-ro)

plums
susine (soo-see-nay)

fruit salad
macedonia (ma-*kay*-do-nee-a)

DESSERTS & CAKES
DOLCI & TORTE

jelly
gelatina *(je-la-tee-na)*

apple pie
torta di mele
(tohr-ta dee may-lay)

chocolate cake
torta di cioccolato *(tohr-ta dee chok-ko-la-to)*

sponge cake with custard and cream
zuppa inglese
(tsoop-pa eeng-lay-say)

sponge cake with cream cheese, chocolate and candied fruit
cassata siciliana *(ka-saa-ta see-chee-lee-a-na)*

sponge cake with mascarpone, eggs and chocolate
tiramisù
(tee-ra-mee-soo)

soufflé with ricotta and candied fruit
budino di ricotta *(boo-dee-no dee ree-ko-tta)*

chestnut cake with sultanas, pine nuts
castagnaccio
(kas-tan-ya-cho)

cinnamon custard
lattaiolo *(lat-ta-yo-lo)*

biscuits
biscotti *(bees-ko-tee)*

Christmas sponge cake
pandoro *(pan-doh-ro)*

Christmas bread with candied fruit
panettone
(pa-neh-tto-nay)

nut and honey cake
pangiallo *(pan-gee-a-llo)*

Italian blancmange and crème brûlée
panna cotta
(pahn-nah kot-ta)

rich fruit cake with figs and honey
pestingolo
(pes-teen-go-lo)

layered cake with meringue, fresh fruit and whipped cream
torta margherita
(tohr-ta mar-gay-ree-ta)

MONEY MATTERS
AFFARI DI DENARO

bureau de change
cambiavalute/cambio
*(kam-bee-a-va-loo-teh/
kam-bee-o)*

cash dispenser/ATM
cassa automatica/
bancomat *(kas-sa ow-to-
ma-tee-ka/ban-ko-mat)*

**Where can I change
money?**
Dove posso cambiare
denaro?
*(do-veh pos-so kam-
bee-aa-ray de-naa-ro)*

Where is ...?
Dov'è ...? *(do-veh)*

- ◆ **an ATM, a cash
  machine, a bank**
- ◆ il bancomat, la cassa
  automatica, una banca
  *(eel ban-ko-mat, la
  kas-sa ow-to-ma-tee-
  ka, oo-na ban-ka)*

**When does the bank
open/close?**
Quando apre/chiude la
banca?*(kwan-do a-pray/
kee-oo-day la ban-ka)*

**How much commis-
sion do you charge?**
Quanto prendete di
commissione?
*(kwan-to pren-deh-teh
dee ko-mee-see-o-ne)*

I want to ...
Voglio/vorrei ...
(vol-yo/ vor-reh-ee ...)

- ◆ **cash a traveller's
  cheque**
- ◆ riscuotere un assegno
  di viaggio
  *(rees-kwo-tere oon
  a-ssen-yo dee vee-a-jo)*

- ◆ **change £50**
- ◆ cambiare cinquanta
  sterline *(kam-bee-a-ray
  chin-kwan-ta
  stayr-lee-nay)*

- ◆ **make a transfer**
- ◆ trasferire soldi
  (tras-fer-ee-ray sol-dee)

POST OFFICE
UFFICIO POSTALE

How much is ...?
Quanto costa ...?
(kwan-to kos-ta)

- ◆ a letter to ...
- ◆ una lettera per ...
  (<u>oo</u>-na let-te-<u>rah</u> pehr)

- ◆ a small parcel to ...
- ◆ un pacchetto per ...
  (oon pa-<u>ket</u>-to pehr)

Where can I buy stamps?
Dove posso comperare dei francobolli? *(do-<u>veh</u> pos-so kom-pe-ra-<u>ray</u> day fran-ko-bol-<u>lee</u>)*

SHOPPING
FARE COMPERE

What does it cost?
Quanto costa?
(<u>kwan</u>-to <u>kos</u>-ta)

What is the total?
Quant'è in tutto?
(kwan-<u>tay</u> in <u>too</u>-tto)

Where do I pay?
Dove si paga?
(do-<u>veh</u> see pa-<u>ja</u>)

I need a receipt
Ho bisogno di una ricevuta *(o <u>bee</u>-soy-no <u>dee</u> oo-na <u>ree</u>-ce-<u>voo</u>-ta)*

Do you accept credit cards?
Accetta carte di credito? *(a-<u>chet</u>-<u>tah</u> <u>kaar</u>-te dee kre-<u>dee</u>-to)*

Do you take traveller's cheques?
Accetta assegni di viaggio? *(a-<u>chet</u>-<u>tah</u> a-<u>ssen</u>-yee dee <u>vee</u>-a-jo)*

Do you need a deposit?
Debbo pagare un deposito in anticipo? *(dehb-boh pa-<u>jaa</u>-ray oon deh-po-<u>see</u>-toh in an-<u>tee</u>-<u>chee</u>-po)*

Can you wrap it up for me?
Può farmi un pacchetto regalo? *(pwo <u>faar</u>-mi oon pa-ketto re-<u>gaa</u>-lo)*

VAT
I.V.A. (imposta sul valore aggiunto)
(<u>eem</u>-pos-ta <u>sool</u> va-lo-ray a-<u>jee</u>-<u>oon</u>-to)

This is not what I want
Non è quello che voglio *(non eh <u>kway</u>-llo kay vo-<u>lee</u>-o)*

This isn't correct (bill)
Questo è sbagliato
(_kwes_-to eh _zbal_-_yaa_-to)

I want my money back
Voglio un rimborso (_vol_-yo oon _reem_-bor-so)

This is ...
Questo è ... (_kwes_-to eh)

◆ **broken**
◆ rotto (roht-_to_)

◆ **damaged**
◆ guasto (_gwaas_-to)

BUYING CLOTHES
COMPRARE VESTIARIO

Can I try this on?
Posso provarlo?
(_pos_-so pro-_vaar_-lo)

It is too ...
E' troppo (eh _troh_-po)

◆ **big**
◆ grande (_gran_-day)

◆ **small**
◆ piccolo (_pee_-ko-lo)

◆ **tight**
◆ stretto (stre-_ttoh_)

◆ **wide**
◆ largo (_laar_-goh)

◆ **expensive**
◆ caro (_kaa_-ro)

◆ **fragile, delicate**
◆ fragile, delicato
(fra-_jee_-le, de-_lee_-ka-to)

I'll take ...
Prendo ...(pren-_doh_ ...)

◆ **this one**
◆ questo
(_kwes_-to)

◆ **two**
◆ due (_doo_-e)

GROCERY SHOPPING
COMPERE DI DROGHERIA

Where can I buy ...?
Dove posso comperare ...?
(do-_veh_ _pos_-so kom-pe-ra-ray)

◆ **bread**
◆ pane (_paa_-neh)

◆ **rolls**
◆ panini (pa-_nee_-nee)

- **cake**
- torta (_tohr_-tah)

- **cheese**
- formaggio (for-ma-_jee_-o)

- **butter**
- burro (_boo_-rro)

- **milk**
- latte (_laat_-tay)

- **water**
- acqua minerale (_ak_-wa mee-ne-_ra_-le)

- **wine**
- vino (_vee_-no)

- **sparkling wine**
- vino frizzante (_vee_-no free-_saan_-te)

- **beer**
- birra (_bee_-rra)

- **fruit juice**
- succo di frutta (_soo_-ko dee _froo_-tta)

- **meat**
- carne (_kaar_-ne)

- **ham**
- prosciutto (pro-_shoo_-tto)

- **polony, cold meats**
- mortadella, salumi (mor-tah-_day_-la, sa-_loo_-mee)

- **fruit**
- frutta (_froo_-tta)

- **vegetables**
- verdure (ver-_doo_-re)

- **eggs**
- uova (_wo_-va)

I'll take ...
Prendo ... (pren-_doh_ ...)

- **one kilo**
- un chilo (oon _kee_-lo)

- **three slices**
- tre fette (treh fet-teh)

- **a portion of**
- una porzione di (_oo_-na port-see-_o_-ne dee)

- **a packet of**
- un pacchetto di (_oon_ _pa_-ket-to dee)

- **a can/tin of**
- una scatola di (_oo_-na ska-to-_lah_ dee)

- **a bottle of**
- una bottiglia di (_oo_-na bo-_tteel_-ya dee)

CLOTHING SIZES – TAGLIE

Women's Wear – Abbigliamento femminile

UK	Cont. Europe	USA
10	36	8
12	38	10
14	40	12
16	42	14
18	44	16

Menswear – Abbigliamento maschile

UK	Cont. Europe	USA
36	46	36
38	48	38
40	50	40
42	52	42
44	54	44
46	56	46

Men's Shirts – Camicie da uomo

UK	Cont. Europe	USA
14	36	14
14.5	37	14.5
15	38	15
15.5	39	15.5
16	40	16
17	42	17

Shoes – Scarpe

UK	Cont. Europe	USA
5	38	6
6	39	7
7	41	8
8	42	9
9	43	10
10	44	11
11	45	12

SIGHTSEEING
GIRI TURISTICI

Tourist Office
Ufficio turistico (<u>oo</u>-<u>fee</u>-chee-o too-<u>rees</u>-tee-ko)

Do you have brochures/leaflets?
Avete degli opuscoli?
(a-ve-<u>teh</u> <u>day</u>-lee o-<u>poos</u>-ko-lee)

I/We want to visit ...
Voglio/vogliamo visitare ...
(<u>vol</u>-yo/vol-<u>yee</u>-a-mo vee-<u>see</u>-ta-ray)

When is it open/ closed?
Quando apre/chiude?
(<u>kwan</u>-do a-<u>pray</u>/kee-<u>oo</u>-day)

What does it cost?
Quanto costa?
(<u>kwan</u>-to <u>kos</u>-ta)

Are there any reductions for ...?
Ci sono riduzioni/tariffe speciali per ...? (chee <u>so</u>-no ree-doo-tsee-<u>o</u>-nee/ ta-<u>ree</u>-fay spe-kee-<u>ah</u>-lee pehr)

♦ **children**
♦ bambini
   (bam-<u>bee</u>-nee)

♦ **senior citizens**
♦ anziani
   (ant-<u>see</u>-a-nee)

♦ **students**
♦ studenti
   (<u>stoo</u>-den-tee)

Are there any tours?
Ci sono delle visite turistiche? (chee <u>so</u>-no day-la vee-<u>see</u>-teh too-<u>ree</u>-stee-ke)

Where/when does the coach/bus depart/return?
Da dove/quando parte/ritorna il pullman?
(dah do-<u>veh</u>/<u>kwan</u>-do par-tay/ree-<u>tor</u>-na eel poolman)

Where is the museum?
Dov'è il museo?
(do-veh eel <u>moo</u>-se-o)

How much is the entrance fee?
Quanto costa l'entrata?
(<u>kwan</u>-to <u>kos</u>-ta len-<u>traa</u>-ta)

ENTERTAINMENT
DIVERTIMENTO

Is there a list of cultural events?
C'è una lista degli eventi culturali? *(che oo-na lees-ta day-lee e-ven-tee kool-too-raa-lee)*

Are there any festivals?
Ci sono dei festival? *(chee so-no day fes-tee-val)*

I would like to go to ...
Vorrei andare ... *(vor-re-hee aan-da-ray ...)*

◆ **the theatre**
◆ al teatro *(al tee-a-tro)*

◆ **the opera**
◆ all'opera *(all-o-pe-rah)*

◆ **the ballet**
◆ al balletto *(al bal-leh-tto)*

◆ **the cinema/movies**
◆ al cinema *(al chee-ne-ma)*

◆ **a concert**
◆ un concerto *(oon kon-cher-to)*

Do I have to book?
Bisogna prenotare? *(bi-son-ya pre-no-taa-ray)*

How much are the tickets?
Quanto costano i biglietti? *(kwan-to kos-taa-no ee beel-yay-ttee)*

Two tickets for ...
Due biglietti per ... *(doo-ay beel-yay-ttee pehr ...)*

◆ **tonight**
◆ questa sera *(kwes-ta seh-ra)*

◆ **tomorrow night**
◆ domani sera *(do-maa-nee seh-ra)*

◆ **the early show**
◆ lo spettacolo del pome riggio *(lo spe-ttaa-ko-loh del po-me-ree-jo)*

◆ **late show**
◆ spettacolo serale *(spe-ttaa-ko-loh se-ra-lay)*

When does the performance start/end?
Quando incomincia/finisce lo spettacolo? *(kwan-do een-ko-meen-cha/fee-nee-shay lo spe-ttaa-ko-loh)*

Where is ...?
Dov'è ...? *(do-__veh__)*

- ◆ **a good bar**
- ◆ un buon bar
  (oon bwon bar)

- ◆ **good live music**
- ◆ una buona orchestra
  (__oo__-na __bwo__-na or-__kes__-tra)

Is it ...?
È ...? *(eh)*

- ◆ **expensive**
- ◆ caro *(__ka__-ro)*

- ◆ **noisy**
- ◆ rumoroso
  (roo-mo-__ro__-so)

- ◆ **crowded**
- ◆ affollato *(a-ffo-__llaa__-to)*

How do I get there?
Come ci si arriva? *(__ko__-may chee see a-__rree__-va)*

SPORT
SPORT

Where can we ...?
Dove possiamo ...?
(do-__veh__ po-__ssee__-a-mo)

- ◆ **play tennis/golf**
- ◆ giocare a tennis/golf
  (jee-o-__kaa__-ray ah tennis/golf)

- ◆ **go skiing**
- ◆ sciare *(shee-a-__ray__)*

- ◆ **go swimming**
- ◆ nuotare *(nwo-__taa__-ray)*

- ◆ **go fishing**
- ◆ pescare *(pe-__shaa__-ray)*

- ◆ **go riding**
- ◆ andare a cavallo *(__aan__-da-ray ah ka-__val__-lo)*

- ◆ **go cycling**
- ◆ andare in bicicletta
  (__aan__-da-ray in __bee__-__chee__-klet-te)

- ◆ **hire bicycles**
- ◆ noleggiare biciclette
  (no-lay-__djaa__-ray __bee__-__chee__-klet-te)

- ◆ **hire tackle**
- ◆ noleggiare articoli per la pesca *(no-lay-__djaa__-ray ar-__tee__-ko-lee pehr la __pe__-sha)*

- ◆ **hire golf clubs**
- ◆ noleggiare mazze da golf *(no-lay-__djaa__-ray __mat__-seh da golf)*

- **hire skis**
- noleggiare sci
  (*no-lay-djaa-ray shee*)

- **hire a boat**
- noleggiare una barca
  (*no-lay-djaa-ray oo-na bar-ka*)

- **hire skates**
- noleggiare pattini
  (*no-lay-djaa-ray pa-ttee-nee*)

- **hire an umbrella**
- noleggiare un ombrello
  (*no-lay-djaa-ray oon om-breh-llo*)

- **hire a deck chair**
- noleggiare una sedia
  a sdraio (*no-lay-djaa-ray oo-na se-dee-a ah sdraa-ee-o*)

How much is it ...?
Quanto costa ...?
(*kwan-to kos-ta*)

- **per hour**
- all'ora (*a-llo-rah*)

- **per day**
- al giorno (*al jor-no*)

- **per session/game**
- alla partita
  (*al-la par-tee-ta*)

Is it ...?
È ...? (*eh*)

- **safe**
- sicuro (*see-koo-ro*)

- **deep**
- profondo (*pro-fon-doh*)

- **clean**
- pulito (*poo-lee-to*)

How do we get there?
Come ci si arriva? (*ko-may chee see a-rree-va*)

no swimming/diving
vietato nuotare/tuffarsi
(*vee-ay-ta-to nwo-ta-ray/too-ffar-see*)

Are there currents?
Ci sono correnti? (*chee so-no co-rren-tee*)

Do I need a fishing permit?
Ho bisogno di un permesso per la pesca? (*o bee-son-yo dee oon per-meh-sso pehr la pe-sha*)

Where can I get one?
Dove posso trovarlo?
(*do-veh pos-so tro-vaar-loh*)

Is there a guide for walks?

C'è una guida per le escursioni a piedi? *(che oo-na gwee-da pehr lay es-koor-see-o-nee ah pee-ay-dee)*

Do I need walking boots?

Ho bisogno di scarponi speciali? *(o bee-son-yo dee skar-po-nee spe-kee-a-lee)*

How much is a ski pass?

Quanto costa una tessera per sciare? *(kwan-to kos-ta oo-na te-sse-rah pehr shee-a-ray)*

Is it safe to ski today?

È sicuro sciare oggi? *(eh see-koo-ro shee-a-ray o-jee)*

I'm a beginner

Sono un principiante *(so-no oon preen-chee-pee-an-te)*

Which is an easy run?

Quale è una pista facile? *(kwa-le eh oo-na pees-ta fa-chee-le)*

My skis are too long/short

Questi sci sono troppo lunghi/corti *(kwes-tee schee so-no troh-ppo loon-gee/kor-tee)*

run closed

pista chiusa *(pees-ta kee-oo-sa)*

avalanches

valanghe *(va-lang-geh)*

We want to go …

Noi vogliamo andare a … *(noy vol-yee-a-mo aan-da-ray ah …)*

◆ **hiking**
◆ fare escursionismo a piedi *(faa-ray es-koor-see-o-nees-mo ah pee-ay-dee*

◆ **sailing**
◆ fare vela *(faa-ray veh-lah)*

◆ **ice-skating**
◆ pattinare su ghiaccio *(pa-ttee-na-ray soo gee-a-cho)*

◆ **water-skiing**
◆ fare lo sci acquatico *(faa-ray lo shee ak-wa-tee-ko)*

PHARMACY/ CHEMIST
FARMACIA

Chains for toiletries, etc. and some medicines not on prescription
Articoli da toilette e senza ricetta medicina
(ar-_tee_-ko-lee da toy-let-te eh sen-sa _ree_-chet-ta me-_dee_-_chee_-na)

health shop
il negozio di cibi naturali
(eel ne-got-_see_-o _dee_ _chee_-bee na-too-_raa_-lee)

Have you got something for ...?
Avete qualche rimedio per ...? (a-_veh_-teh _kwal_-ke _ree_-me-_dee_-o pehr ...)

◆ car sickness
◆ il mal d'auto
  (eel mal _dow_-to)

◆ diarrhoea
◆ la diarrea
  (la _dee_-ay-rrea)

◆ a headache
◆ il mal di testa
  (eel mal dee _tes_-tah)

◆ a sore throat
◆ il mal di gola
  (eel mat dee goh-_lah_)

◆ stomachache
◆ il mal di stomaco (eel mal dee sto-_maa_-ko)

◆ a cold or flu
◆ raffreddore o l'influenza
  (raff-re-ddo-reh o _leen_-floo-_en_-sa)

I need ...
Ho bisogno di ...
(o _bee_-son-yo _dee_ ...)

◆ indigestion tablets
◆ pillole per indigestione
  (_peel_-lo-le pehr _een_-dee-_ges_-tee-o-ne)

◆ laxative
◆ lassativo (las-_saa_-_tee_-vo)

◆ sleeping tablets
◆ pillole per dormire (_peel_-lo-le pehr dor-_mee_-ray)

◆ a painkiller
◆ un analgesico
  (oon an-al-je-_see_-ko)

Is it safe for children?
Va bene per bambini?
(vah be-_nay_ pehr bam-_bee_-nee)

I'm a diabetic
Sono diabetico/a (*so-no dee-a-be-tee-ko/a*)

I'm pregnant
Sono incinta
(*so-no een-cheen-ta*)

allergic
allergico/a (*aller-jee-ko/a*)

DOCTOR
DOTTORE

I am ill
Sono ammalato/a
(*so-no am-ma-laa-to/a*)

I need a doctor
Ho bisogno di un dottore
(*o bee-son-yo dee oon do-tto-reh*)

He/she has high temperature
Lui/lei ha la febbre alta
(*loo-ee/lay a la feb-bray al-tah*)

It hurts
Fa male (*fa maa-leh*)

I'm going to be sick!
Ho voglia di vomitare!
(*o vol-yo dee vo-mee-taa-ray*)

Dentist
il/la dentista
(*eel/la den-tees-ta*)

I have toothache
Ho mal di denti
(*o mal dee den-tee*)

Ophthalmologist
l'oftalmologo/a
(*lof-tal-moh-lo-jo/a*)

HOSPITAL
OSPEDALE

Will I have to go to hospital?
Debbo andare all'ospedale?
(*deb-boh an-daa-ray al-los-pe-daa-lay*)

Where is the hospital?
Dov'è l'ospedale?
(*do-veh los-pe-daa-lay*)

Which ward?
Quale sala?
(*kwaa-le saa-la*)

When are visiting hours?
Quando sono le ore di visita? (*kwan-do so-no le o-ray vee-see-ta*)

Where is casualty?
Dov'è il pronto soccorso?
(do-_veh_ eel _pron_-to so-kkor-_soh_)

POLICE
LA POLIZIA

Call the police
Chiami la polizia (kee-_aa_-mee la po-_leet_-see-a)

I have been robbed
Sono stato derubato (_so_-no _sta_-to de-roo-_baa_-to)

My car has been stolen
La mia macchina è stata rubata
(la _mee_-a _ma_-kkee-na eh _sta_-ta roo-_baa_-ta)

My car has been broken into
Hanno rubato nella mia macchina
(an-no roo-_baa_-to nella _mee_-a _ma_-kkee-na)

I have been attacked
Sono stato assalito (_so_-no _sta_-to ass-al-_eet_-o)

I want to report a theft
Voglio denunciare un furto (_vol_-yo de-_noon_-_chee_-a-ray oon _foor_-to)

Where is the police station?
Dov'è la stazione di polizia? (do-_veh_ la sta-tsy-_o_-ne dee po-_leet_-see-a)

EMERGENCIES
EMERGENZE

Call an ambulance!
Chiami un'ambulanza!
(kee-_aa_-mee _oon_-am-boo-_lant_-sa)

There's been an accident
C'è stato un incidente
(cheh _sta_-to oon _een_-_chee_-_den_-te)

Someone is injured
C'è un ferito (cheh oon fe-_ree_-to)

Hurry up!
Presto! (_pres_-toh)

Help!
Aiuto! *(a-ee-oo-to)*

Could you please help me?
Per favore, mi aiuti?
(pehr fa-vo-ray, mee a-ee-oo-tee)

My son/daughter is missing
Mio figlio/figlia è smarrita
(mee-o/mee-a fee-lee-yo/ fee-lee-ya eh sma-rree-ta)

This is an emergency!
C'è un'emergenza!
(cheh oon-em-er-gen-sa)

I need a report for my insurance
Devo avere un rapporto per la mia assicurazione
(day-vo a-veh-reh oon rap-po-roh pehr la mee-a a-ssee-koo-rat-see-o-nay)

I want to phone my embassy
Voglio telefonare alla mia ambasciata
(vol-yo tay-lay-fo-naa-re al-lah mee-a am-ba-sshee-a-ta)

I am lost
Sono perduto
(so-no per-doo-to)

FIRE DEPARTMENT
CORPO DEI VIGILI DEL FUOCO

Fire!
Fuoco!
(fwo-ko)

Look out!
Attenzione!
(a-tten-see-o-nay)

Call the fire department
Chiami i vigili del fuoco
(kee-aa-mee ee vee-jee-lee del fwo-ko)

The address is ...
L'indirizzo è ...
(leen-dee-ree-tso eh ...)

I need ...
Ho bisogno di ...
(o bee-son-yo dee ...)

◆ **a fire extinguisher**
◆ un estintore
(oon es-teen-to-re)

◆ **medical assistance**
◆ assistenza medica
(a-ssees-tent-sa me-dee-cha)

THE HUMAN BODY
IL CORPO UMANO

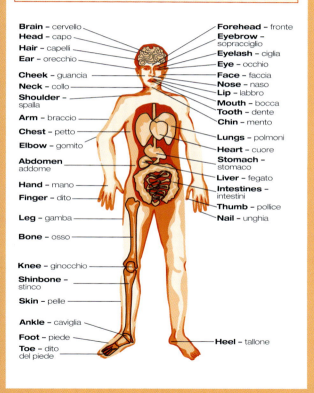

Brain – cervello

Head – capo

Hair – capelli

Ear – orecchio

Cheek – guancia

Neck – collo

Shoulder – spalla

Arm – braccio

Chest – petto

Elbow – gomito

Abdomen addome

Hand – mano

Finger – dito

Leg – gamba

Bone – osso

Knee – ginocchio

Shinbone – stinco

Skin – pelle

Ankle – caviglia

Foot – piede

Toe – dito del piede

Forehead – fronte

Eyebrow – sopracciglio

Eyelash – ciglia

Eye – occhio

Face – faccia

Nose – naso

Lip – labbro

Mouth – bocca

Tooth – dente

Chin – mento

Lungs – polmoni

Heart – cuore

Stomach – stomaco

Liver – fegato

Intestines – intestini

Thumb – pollice

Nail – unghia

Heel – tallone

FORMS OF ADDRESS
FORME PER RIVOLGERSI A QUALCUNO

Signorina (Miss) is rarely used in Italy today and is best avoided, unless a woman appears relatively young and you are unsure of her marital status. Generally speaking, *Signore* (for a man) and *Signora* (for a woman) are the safest options. A male university graduate is given the title of *Dottore*, and *Dottoressa* is the female equivalent. If you need to call a waiter, use the word *senta*, which means 'please come here'.

Frequent and vigorous handshakes can be common on social occasions. Upon arrival and departure, shake hands with everyone individually in a group, as one general 'hello' or 'goodbye' to the group will not really be appreciated. Italians will not hesitate to greet people they know with an embrace, usually kissing each other once on each cheek – this applies to both males and females.

In stores or restaurants, it is a courtesy to greet people with an appropriate greeting when you arrive and when you leave. *Buon giorno* on arrival and *arrivederci* as you leave are the appropriate greetings.

MANNERS
MANIERE

Younger people should give up their seats to older people on public transport. Chewing, leaning and slouching are unacceptable in public, and you should also avoid raising your hand or fingers. On the other hand, gentle pushing and shoving in queues is a common occurrence in Italy.

Some typically Italian gestures may need to be explained. Touching your nose indicates confidentiality. Pointing with the index and little finger is a gesture used when wishing someone bad luck. Placing the hand on the stomach indicates dislike for someone. Slapping your raised arm above the elbow and thumbing your nose are both considered to be very offensive gestures.

APPROPRIATE DRESS
ABITO ADATTO

It is important to know what to wear in a business environment. Men should wear tailored dark suits and sophisticated ties – quality fabrics such as lightweight wools and silks are customary. Cuff links add to the sophistication, as do tie clips and watches. Italians generally use aftershaves of the highest quality, but not too much.

Women are advised to dress for business with elegant simplicity, and to accessorize with jewellery. Darker, subdued shades are most commonly worn, with brighter colours used for accessories. Perfumes are very popular. It is fashionable, especially in sum- mer, for women not to wear stockings.

Although leisure wear is less formal, shorts are unacceptable in public and you will not be allowed into a church if you are wearing shorts or a sleeveless top. On the street, jeans and sneakers are accepted as leisure wear, although this kind of clothing is mainly for the gym or the beach.

When it comes to social occasions, your clothing will be perceived as a reflection of your social standing and relative success. Informal dress does not exist in Italy, so even if you receive an invitation stating 'informal' dress, do not embarrass yourself by arriving in sweatpants and a T-shirt. 'Informal' means tastefully coordinated clothes, including a jacket and tie. An invitation stating 'formal' would mean that you should don your very best dressy evening wear.

Clothes should always be stylish, chosen with good taste and not be gaudy. Quality and labels are important factors as the Italians are very fashion-conscious. Dark, discreet colours in the best fabrics – like silk – are the way to go.

COMMUNICATION
COMUNICAZIONI

Italian communication is highly emotive, eloquent and tends to be very animated, so expect to be interrupted!

Communication tends to be quieter in a business setting The authority figure will not have to raise his or her voice as this is an individual who is used to being noticed and listened to.

Trust is very important to Italians. This is why they prefer to do business with people they have already met. First impressions are also important, so be sure to make eye contact immediately when being introduced to someone. Italians show their interest with sustained eye contact.

In Italian culture, people are traditionally expected to behave with a sense of decorum and formality at all times. This concept is known as *Bella Figura* ('beautiful figure'), which generally means presenting yourself well, especially when communicating.

HIERARCHY AND RESPECT
ORDINE DI PRECEDENZA E RISPETTO

A person's position and influence within an organization, as well as their achievements, are of great importance to Italians. Both in a business environment and in family life, a hierarchical structure is strictly adhered to. Much respect is given to those higher in command and age.

Although women generally receive a lot of respect from men in Italy, they are still not given equal rights and similar positions when it comes to business.

Italians are a proud nation. Never insult an Italian's honour or that of his or her friends and family. Also don't make any negative remarks about the area in which they live. That said, Italians are usually responsive to constructive criticism, as long as it is presented in such a way that they are able to retain their pride and dignity.

Italians very rarely speak to each other on a first-name basis in business, so only use their Christian name if you have been told to do so. Complementing employees in public is definitely not standard procedure.

Punctuality is appreciated for business meetings, but you should not be offended if you are kept waiting by your host. Make sure you always close doors behind you and knock before entering.

Religion is a very important part of life in Italy, so make sure that you never blaspheme and swear.

DINING FORMALITIES
FORMALITÀ DI PRANZARE

Behaving incorrectly when having a business lunch could have serious consequences regarding your business deal. You will be thought to be impolite if you leave the table during the meal unless absolutely necessary, even if you are going to the toilet.

The person who is perceived to be the most important is usually seated to the right of the host and at the center of the side of the table. It is quite common for couples to be spilt up – this is done to help improve conversation among those people who have not met each other before.

If you are the person who has invited your business associates for a meal, you should collect the bill.

Wines are sipped at leisure and for the purpose of enjoyment, not for getting drunk. You will seldom find Italians getting drunk.

If you are offered more food than you wish to consume, you can decline politely, but you may have to be prepared to insist. Italians are very generous when it comes to their food and you might not be believed when you say you have had enough.

In Italy it is offensive to raise your fingers or hands to gain the waiter's attention. The best way is to make eye contact with him or gesture with your palm facing the floor.

When invited to a meal at someone's home, it is appropriate to bring a gift like chocolates or flowers for the hostess. It is also a good idea to follow up with a phone call the next day.

OFFICIAL HOLIDAYS 85
FESTE UFFICIALI 85

REGIONAL HOLIDAYS 86
FESTE REGIONALI 86

NATIONAL DAY 86
GIORNATA NAZIONALE 86

SPECIAL FESTIVALS 86
FESTIVAL SPECIALI 86

OFFICIAL HOLIDAYS
FESTE UFFICIALI

New Year's Day
Capodanno or *Primo dell'Anno* (1 January)
Great festivities are held throughout Italy.

Epiphany
Epifania (6 January)
A religious holiday.

Easter Monday
Lunedì di Pasqua
The day after Easter is spent with the family decorating and eating hard-boiled eggs, as well as chocolate eggs and traditional Easter cake (*Colomba Pasquale*), a sponge cake in the shape of a dove representing peace and harmony.

Liberation Day
Anniversario della Liberazione (25 April)
A public holiday celebrating the liberation of Italy in 1945.

Labour Day
Festa del Lavoro (1 May)
A day off for workers.

Assumption Day
Ferragosto (15 August)
A religious holiday.

All Saints' Day
Ognissanti (1 November)
A religious holiday in honour of the saints.

Immaculate Conception
L'immacolata Concezione (8 December)
A religious holiday.

Christmas Day
Natale (25 December)
Celebrated with church services and the giving of gifts.

St Stephen's Day
Santo Stefano
(26 December)
The day after Christmas is a public holiday, usually spent with the family.

REGIONAL HOLIDAYS
FESTE REGIONALI

Each region, town and village in Italy has its own holiday and annual festival. These festivals are usually in summer and are held in honour of the local patron saint.

NATIONAL DAY
GIORNATA NAZIONALE

Anniversary of the Republic *Festa della Repubblica* (2 June)
Italy's National Day.

SPECIAL FESTIVALS
FESTIVAL SPECIALI

Carnevale
Carnival is a joyous celebration consisting of various kinds of merrymaking and festivities. It takes place throughout the country during the last few days before the commencement of the austere 40 days of Lent, which precedes Easter in the Christian calendar.

il Palio di Siena

(usually on 26 August)

Siena's Palio starts with a grand historical parade of people in medieval costumes. This takes place in the *Campo* (main square) of Siena. The festival closes with a reckless bareback horse race around the square in which the 17 different districts of the town compete for the final prize, the *palio* – a prestigious hand-painted banner.

Stagione Lirica del l'arena di Verona

(July to August)

This is Verona's annual open-air opera festival. Various operas are performed on the enormous stage of the Arena – a Roman Amphitheatre. The arena is so big that live elephants can be used on stage for performances of Verdi's *Aïda*.

Ferragosto

(August holidays)

Centred around the 15th of August, this holiday period at the height of summer is observed nationally. All factories close down and everyone goes on holiday to the seaside, to the mountains and to the lakes. Roads are congested during this period and holiday resorts are usually very crowded.

ENGLISH → ITALIAN

A

abbey abbazia f
abortion aborto m
about (approximately)
  circa
above sopra
abroad all'estero
abscess ascesso m
absolutely
  assolutamente
accelerator
  acceleratore m
accent accento m
accept accettare
accident incidente m
accommodation
  alloggio m
account conto m
accurate preciso/a
ache dolore m
adapter adattatore m
adhesive tape
  nastro adesivo m
admission fee quota
  d'entrata
adult (adj, n)
  adulto/a m/f
advance, in advance
  anticipo m,
  anticipatamente
advert, advertisement
  pubblicità f
advise avvisare
aeroplane
  aeroplano m
afraid, afraid of paura,
  paura di
after dopo

afternoon
  pomeriggio m
afterwards in seguito
again di nuovo
against contro
age età f
ago, a week ago fa,
  una settimana fa
agree accordarsi
agreement accordo m
air aria f
air conditioning aria
  condizionata
air ticket biglietto
  aereo m
airmail posta aerea f
airport aeroporto m
aisle corridoio m
aisle seat posto sul
  corridoio
all right va bene
allow permettere
almond mandorla f
almost quasi
alone solo
already già
also anche
although benchè,
  sebbene
altogether in tutto
always sempre
a.m. (before noon)
  antimeridiane,
  del mattino
am, I am sono, io sono
amazing incredibile
amber ambra f

ambulance ambulanza **f**

among tra

amount quantità **f**

anaesthetic anestesia **f**

ancient antico/a

and e

angry arrabbiato/a

animal animale **m**

ankle caviglia **f**

anniversary anniversario **m**

annoy dare fastidio

annual annuale

another un altro

answer risposta **f**

ant formica **f**

antacid antiacido

anybody chiunque

anything qualche cosa, qualcosa

apartment appartamento **m**

appendicitis appendicite **f**

apology scusa **f**

appointment appuntamento **m**

apron grembiule **m**

are sono

area area **f**

armchair poltrona **f**

arrange sistemare

arrest (n) arresto **m**

arrest (vb) arrestare

arrival arrivo **m**

art arte **f**

artist artista **f**

ask domandare

astonishing stupefacente

at a

attack (n) attacco **m**

attack (vb) attaccare, assalire

attic soffitta **f**

audience pubblico **m**

aunt zia **f**

auto-teller sportello automatico

autumn autunno **m**

available disponibile

avalanche valanga **f**

avenue viale **m**

average mediocre

avoid evitare

awake sveglio

away via

awful brutto/a

B

baby buggy passeggino **m**

baby food cibo per bambini, alimenti per l'infanzia

back schiena **f**

backache mal di schiena

backpack zaino **m**

bacon pancetta **f**

bad cattivo/a

bag borsa **f**

baggage bagagli **m**

ENGLISH → ITALIAN

baggage reclaim ritiro
   bagagli
bait esca f
bakery panificio m
balcony balcone m
ballpoint pen penna a
   sfera
Baltic Sea il mare
   Baltico
bandage benda f
bar of chocolate
   tavoletta di cioccolato
barber barbiere m
bark (n, of tree)
   corteccia f
bark (vb, dog)
   abbaiare
barn granaio m
barrel barile m
basement
   seminterrato m
basket cestino m
bath bagno m
bathroom camera da
   bagno
Bavaria Baviera
bay baia f
bay leaf foglia d'alloro
be essere
beach spiaggia f
bean fagiolo m
beard barba f
beautiful bello/a
beauty salon istituto di
   bellezza
because perchè
bed letto m

bed & breakfast
   camera con colazione,
   alloggio prima calazione
bee ape f
beef manzo m
before prima di
beginner principiante
behind dietro
Belgium Belgio m
believe credere
bell campanello m
below sotto
belt cintura f
bend curva f
beside accanto
bet (n) scommessa f
bet (vb) scommettere
better meglio
beyond oltre
bicycle bicicletta f
big grande
bill conto m
bin pattumiera f,
   bidone m
binoculars binocoli
bird uccello m
birth nascita f
birth certificate
   certificato di nascita
birthday compleanno m
birthday card biglietto
   di auguri di compleanno
birthday present
   regalo per il compleanno
biscuit biscotto m
bit pezzo m
bite (n) morso m
bite (vb) mordere

ENGLISH → ITALIAN

black nero/a
Black Forest Foresta
  Nera
black ice strato di
  ghiaccio invisibile
blackcurrants ribes
  neri
blanket coperta f
bleach decolorante m
bleed sanguinare
blind (adj) cieco/a
blind (n, for window)
  tenda veneziana f
blister vescica f
block of flats blocco
  di appartamenti m
blocked bloccato
blood sangue m
blood pressure
  pressione del sangue
blouse camicetta f
blow-dry asciugare con
  l'asciugacapelli
blue blu
blunt spuntato/a
blusher rosso per le
  guance
boar cinghiale m
boarding card la carta
  d'imbarco
boarding house
  pensione f
boat nave f
boat trip viaggio in nave
body corpo m
boil (n, med)
  foruncolo m
boil (vb) bollire

bone osso m
bonnet (of car)
  cofano m
book (n) libro m
book (vb, ticket)
  prendere un biglietto per
bookshop libreria f
boot (car)
  portabagagli m
boot (shoe) stivale m
border frontiera f
boring noioso/a
born nato/a
borrow prendere a
  prestito
both tutti e due
bottle bottiglia f
bottle opener
  apribottiglie m
bottom (at the)
  in fondo alla
bow tie cravatta a
  farfalla
bowl scodella f
box scatola f
boy ragazzo m
boyfriend ragazzo,
  amico m
bra reggiseno m
bracelet
  braccialetto m
brake freno m
brake fluid
  liquido per freni
brake light
  luce del freno
branch (office)
  succursale f

brand (n) marca f
brandy cognac m
bread pane m
break rompere
break in entrata forzata
breakable fragile
breakdown (of car) guasto m, panna f
breakdown van carro attrezzi/soccorso
breakfast prima colazione
breast seno m
breathe respirare
breeze brezza f
brewery birreria f
brick mattone m
bride sposa f
bridegroom sposo m
bridge ponte m
briefcase cartella f
bright brillante
bring portare
Britain Gran Bretagna
brochure opuscolo m
broken rotto/a
bronchitis bronchite f
brooch spilla f
broom scopa f
brother fratello m
brother-in-law cognato m
brown marrone
bruise (n) livido m
brush spazzola f
Brussels Bruxelles
bucket secchio m
buffet car vagone

ristorante
build costruire
building edificio m
bulb (elec) lampadina f
bulb (plant) bulbo m
bumper (car) paraurti m
bunch (flowers) mazzo m
bunch (grapes) grappolo m
bureau de change cambiavalute
burglar ladro/a m/f
burglary furto m
burn (n) bruciatura f
burn (vb) bruciare
burst scoppiare
bus autobus m
bus stop fermata d'autobus
bush cespuglio m
business affare m
business trip viaggio d'affari
busy occupato/a
but ma
butcher macellaio m
butter burro m
butterfly farfalla f
button bottone m
buy comprare, comperare
by da (e.g. by author), entro le (time), via (e.g. by sea)
by myself (alone) da solo

bypass (road)
   circonvallazione **f**

C

cab taxi **m**, tassì **m**
cabbage cavolo **m**
cabin cabina **f**
cable car funivia **f**
cake torta **f**
cake shop pasticceria **f**
calculator calcolatrice **f**
calf vitello **m**
call (n) chiamata **f**
call (vb) chiamare
calm calmo/a
camp (vb)
   campeggiare
campsite
   campeggio **m**
can (n, tin) latta **f**,
   lattina **f**, scatola **f**
can (vb, be able to)
   potere
can opener
   apriscatole **f**
Canada Canada
canal canale **m**
cancel cancellare
cancellation
   cancellazione
cancer cancro **m**
candle candela **f**
candy caramella **f**
canoe canoa **f**
cap berretto **m**
capital (money)
   capitale **m**
capital (city) capitale **f**

car macchina **f**
car ferry traghetto **m**
car hire affittare una
   macchina
car insurance
   assicurazione per la
   macchina
car keys chiavi per la
   macchina
car parts i pezzi di
   ricambio
car wash autolavaggio
caravan carovana **f**
caravan site
   campeggio per
   carovane **m**
carburettor
   carburatore **m**
card (birthday card)
   biglietto di auguri
   (per il compleanno)
cardboard cartone **m**
cardigan cardigan **m**
careful cauto/a
caretaker custode **m/f**,
   guardiano **m**
carpenter
   falegname **m**
carpet tappeto **m**
carriage carrozza **f**
carrier bag borsa (per
   la spesa), busta di carta
carrot carota **f**
carry portare
carry-cot lettino
   portatile **m**
carton scatola di
   cartone

ENGLISH → ITALIAN

93

ENGLISH → ITALIAN

case valigia **f**
cash denaro contante
cash desk cassa **f**
cash dispenser
  sportello automatico
cashier cassiere/a **m/f**
cassette cassetta **f**
castle castello **m**
casualty department
  pronto soccorso **m**
cat gatto **m**
catch prendere,
  acchiappare
cathedral cattedrale **f**
Catholic cattolico/a **m/f**
cauliflower
  cavolfiore **m**
cave grotta **f**
CD player lettore di
  compact
ceiling soffitto **m**
celery sedano **m**
cellar cantina **f**
cemetery cimitero **m**
Centigrade
  centigrado **m**
centimetre
  centimetro **m**
central heating
  riscaldamento centrale
central locking
  serratura automatica
centre centro **m**
century secolo **m**
certain certo/a
certainly certamente
certificate certificato **m**
chair sedia **f**

chair lift seggiovia **f**
chambermaid
  cameriera **f**
champagne
  champagne **m**
change (n, coins)
  spiccioli **mpl**
change (vb) cambiare
changing room
  camerino **m,** spogliatoio
  m (for sports)
channel canale **m**
chapel cappella **f**
charcoal carbone di
  legna **m**
charge caricare
charge card carta di
  credito
charter flight volo
  charter
cheap scadente, a buon
  mercato
cheap rate tariffa
  economica
cheaper a più buon
  mercato
check (vb) verificare
check-in fare il check-in,
  accettazione bagagli
cheek guancia **f**
cheering
  acclamazione **f**
Cheers! Salute!
cheese formaggio **m**
chef cuoco **m**
chemist farmacista **f**
cheque assegno **m**

cheque book libretto
degli assegni
cheque card carta
assegni
cherry ciliegia f
chess scacchi m
chest petto m
chest of drawers
cassettone m
chestnut castagna f
chewing gum gomma
da masticare
chicken pollo m
chicken pox varicella f
child bambino/a m/f
child car seat
seggiolino per macchina
chimney camino m
chin mento m
china porcellana f
China Cina f
chips patatine fritte
chives erba cipollina
chocolate
cioccolato m
chocolates (box of)
una scatola di
cioccolatini
choir coro m
choose scegliere
chop (n) costoletta f
chop (vb) tagliare
(a pezzi)
Christian name nome
di battesimo
Christmas Natale m
Christmas Eve La
Vigilia di Natale

church chiesa f
cider sidro m
cigar sigaro m
cigarette sigaretta f
cigarette lighter
accendino m
cinema cinema m
circle cerchio m
cistern cisterna f
citizen cittadino/a m/f
city città f
city centre il centro
della città
class classe f
clean pulito/a
cleaning solution
detergente
cleansing lotion
lozione detergente
clear chiaro/a
clever intelligente
client cliente m
cliff scogliera f
climb scalare, salire,
arrampicarsi
cling film carta
avvolgente adesiva **f**
clinic clinica f
cloakroom
guardaroba f
clock orologio m
close chiudere
cloth tessuto m
clothes vestiti m
clothes line corda
del bucato
clothes peg molletta
da bucato f

ENGLISH → ITALIAN

cloud nuvola f
clutch frizione f
coach (railway)
  vagone m
coal carbone m
coast costa f
coastguard
  guardia costiera
coat cappotto m
coat hanger gruccia f,
  attaccapanni m,
  stampella f
cockroach
  scarafaggio m
cocoa cacao m
coconut noce di cocco
cod merluzzo m
code codice m
coffee caffè m
coil rotolo m
coin moneta f
Coke Coca–cola f
colander colatoio m,
  scola pasta f
cold freddo/a
collapse crollare
collar colletto m
collarbone clavicola f
colleague collega
collect collezionare
collect call telefonare a
  carico del destinatario
cologne acqua di
  colonia f
colour colore m
colour blind daltonico
colour film rullino a
  colori

comb pettine m
come venire
come back ritornare
come in entrare
comedy commedia f
comfortable comodo/a
company compagnia f
compartment
  scompartimento m
compass bussola f
complain lamentarsi
complaint lamentela f
completely
  completamente
composer
  compositore m
compulsory
  obbligatorio/a
computer computer m
concert concerto m
concession
  concessione f
concussion
  commozione cerebrale
condition condizione f
condom preservativo m
conference
  conferenza f
confirm confermare
confirmation
  conferma f
confuse confondere
congratulations
  congratulazioni
connecting flight
  volo coincidenza
connection
  coincidenza f

conscious conscio/a
constipated stitico/a
consulate consolato m
contact (n) contatto m
contact (vb) mettere in contatto
contact lens lenti a contatto
continue continuare
contraceptive contraccettivo, anticoncezionale
contract contratto m
convenient comodo/a
cook (n) cuoco m
cook (vb) cucinare
cooker fornello m
cookie biscotto m
cooking utensils gli utensili da cucina
cool fresco/a
cool bag/box borsa termica f
copy copiare
cork tappo m
corkscrew cavatappi m
corner angolo m
correct corretto/a
corridor corridoio m
cost costo m
cot lettino m
cotton cotone m
cotton wool cotone idrofilo
couch divano m
couchette cuccetta f
cough (n) tosse f

cough (vb) tossire
cough mixture sciroppo per la tosse
could potrei
couldn't non potrei
counter banco m
country paese m
countryside campagna f
couple coppia f
courier service corriere
course corso m
cousin cugino m
cover charge coperto m
cow mucca f
crab granchio m
craft arte f
cramp crampo m
crash (vb) schiantare
crash helmet casco m
cream panna f
crèche asilo, nido m
credit card carta di credito
crime crimine m
crisps patatine fritte
crockery stoviglie f
cross arrabbiato/a
crossing passaggio pedonale
crossroads incrocio m
crossword puzzle parole crociate
crowd folla f
crowded affollato/a
crown corona f

ENGLISH → ITALIAN

ENGLISH → ITALIAN

cruise crociera f
crutches stampelle f
cry piangere
crystal cristallo m
cucumber cetriolo m
cufflinks gemelli m
cup tazza f
cupboard armadio m
curly riccio/a
currency valuta f
current (adj) corrente
current (n) corrente f
curtain tenda f
cushion cuscino m
custard crema pasticciera
custom usanza f
customer cliente m
customs dogana f
cut (n) taglio m
cut (vb) tagliare
cutlery posate
cycle (n) ciclo m
cycle track pista per bicilette
cyst ciste f
cystitis cistite f
Czech Republic Repubblica Ceca

D
daily giornaliero/a
damage (n) danno m
damp umido/a
dance (vb) ballare
danger pericolo m
dangerous pericoloso/a
dark scuro/a

date appuntamento m
date of birth data di nascita
dates datteri m
daughter figlia f
daughter-in-law nuora f
dawn alba f
day giorno m
dead morto/a
deaf sordo/a
deal patto m
dear caro/a
death morte f
debts debiti m
decaffeinated decaffeinato
December dicembre m
decide decidere
decision decisione f
deck chair sedia a sdraio
deduct dedurre
deep profondo/a
definitely sicuramente
degree (measurement) grado m
degree (qualification) laurea f
delay (n) ritardo m
delay (vb) ritardare
deliberately deliberatamente
delicious delizioso/a
deliver consegnare
delivery consegna f
Denmark Danimarca f

dental floss
interdentale
dentist dentista m/f
dentures dentiera
depart partire
department sezione
department store
grande magazzino m
departure partenza f
departure lounge
la sala delle partenze
deposit (n) deposito m
deposit (vb) depositare
describe descrivere
description
descrizione f
desk banco m
dessert dolce m
destination
destinazione f
details particolari m
detergent
detersivo m
detour deviazione f
develop sviluppare
diabetic (adj, n)
diabetico/a m/f
dial (n) quadrante m
dialling code
prefisso m
dialling tone segnale di
linea libera
diamond diamante m
diaper pannolino m
diarrhoea diarrea f
diary agenda f
dice dado m
dictionary dizionario m

die morire
diesel nafta f
diet dieta f
difference
differenza f
different diverso/a
difficult difficile
dinghy canotto
pneumatico
dining room
la sala da pranzo
dinner cena f
direct diretto/a
direction direzione f
directory (phone)
guida telefonica
dirty sporco/a
disabled invalido/a
disappear scomparire
disappointed deluso/a
disaster disastro m
disconnected
staccato/a
discount sconto m
discover scoprire
disease malattia f
dish piatto m
dishtowel
strofinaccio m
dishwasher rondella f
disinfectant
disinfettante m
disk disco m
**disposable diapers/
nappies** pannolini
usa e getta
distance distanza f
district regione f

disturb disturbare
dive (vb) tuffarsi
diving board
  trampolino m
divorced divorziato/a
DIY shop negozio di
  bricolage
dizzy vertiginoso/a
do fare
doctor dottore m
document
  documento m
dog cane m
doll bambola f
domestic domestico/a
door porta f
doorbell campanello
  della porta
doorman portiere m
double doppio/a
double bed letto
  matrimoniale
double room camera
  doppia
doughnut bombolone
downhill in discesa
downstairs
  al piano di sotto
dozen dozzina f
drain tubo di scarico
draught corrente d'aria
draught beer
  birra alla spina
drawer cassetto m
drawing disegno m
dreadful terribile
dress vestito m

dressing (bandage)
  fasciatura f
dressing (salad)
  condimento m
dressing gown
  vestaglia f
dressing room
  camerino m
drill (n) trapano m
drink (n) bevanda f
drink (vb) bere
drinking water
  acqua potabile
drive guidare
driver autista f
driving licence patente
  di guida
drop (n) goccia f
drug (med) droga f
drug (narcotic)
  narcotico m
drunk ubriaco/a
dry asciutto/a
dry cleaner's tintoria
dryer asciugatore
duck anatra f
due dovuto
dull cupo/a
dummy succhiotto m
during durante
dust polvere f
dustbin pattumiera f
duster strofinaccio m
dustpan paletta per la
  spazzatura
Dutch olandese
duty-free esente da
  dogana

ENGLISH → ITALIAN

duvet piumone m
duvet cover fodera
dye tintura f
dynamo dinamo f

E
each ogni
eagle aquila f
ear orecchio m
earache mal d'orecchi
earphones cuffia
earrings orecchini
earth terra f
earthquake terremoto m
east est
Easter, Happy Easter! Pasqua, Buona Pasqua!
Easter egg uovo di Pasqua
easy facile
eat mangiare
EC CE f
economy economia f
economy class classe economia
edge bordo m
eel anguilla f
egg uovo m
either of them l'uno o l'altro
elastic elastico/a
elbow gomito m
electric elettrico/a
electrician elettricista
electricity elettricità f
elevator ascensore m

embassy ambasciata f
emergency emergenza f
emergency exit uscita di sicurezza
empty vuoto/a
end (n) fine f
end (vb) finire
engaged (busy) occupato/a
engaged (to be married) fidanzato/a
engine motore m
engineer ingegnere m
England Inghilterra
English inglese
Englishman/woman inglese m/f
enjoy divertirsi
enlargement ingrandimento m
enough abbastanza f
enquiry domanda f
enquiry desk ufficio informazioni
enter entrare
entrance entrata f
entrance fee quota d'entrata
envelope busta f
epileptic (adj, n) epilettico/a m/f
equipment attrezzatura f
error errore m
escalator scala mobile
escape (n) fuga f
escape (vb) sfuggire

ENGLISH → ITALIAN

ENGLISH → ITALIAN

especially particolarmente

essential essenziale

estate agent agente immobiliare

Estonia Estonia

EU UE f

Europe Europa f

European (adj, n) europeo/a **m/f**

even uguale

evening sera f

eventually finalmente

every, everyone ogni, ognuno

everything tutto

everywhere dappertutto

exactly esattamente

examination esame m

example, for example esempio m, per esempio

excellent eccellente

except eccetto

excess luggage bagaglio in eccedenza

exchange scambiare

exciting eccitante

exclude escludere

excursion escursione f

excuse me scusi

exhaust pipe tubo di scappamento m

exhausted esausto/a

exhibition mostra f

exit uscita f

expect aspettare, aspettarsi

expenses spese fpl

expensive caro/a

experienced esperto/a

expire scadere

explain spiegare

explosion esplosione f

export esportare

exposure esposizione f

express espresso/a

extension prolungamento m

extension lead prolunga

extra più

extraordinary straordinario/a

eye occhio m

eye drops goccie per gli occhi

eye make-up remover detergente per trucco

eye shadow ombretto m

eyeglasses occhiali m

F

face faccia f

factory fabbrica f

faint (vb) svenire

fair (fête) fiera f

fair (hair colour) biondo/a

fair (just) giusto/a

fairly con giustizia, in modo imparziale

fake (adj) falso/a
fake (n) imitazione f
fall cadere
false falso/a
family famiglia f
famous famoso/a
fan ventilatore m
fan belt cinghia del ventilatore
far lontano/a
fare tariffa f
farm fattoria f
farmer agricoltore m
farmhouse casa colonica
fashionable di moda
fast veloce
fasten allacciare
fasten seatbelt allacciare la cintura di sicurezza
fat grasso/a
father padre m
father-in-law suocero m
fatty grasso/a, grassoccio/a
fault difetto m
faulty difettoso/a
favourite preferito/a
fax fax
February febbraio m
feed (vb) nutrire
feel sentire
feet piedi mpl
female femmina f
fence recinto m
fender parafango m

ferry traghetto m
festival festa f, festival m
fetch andare/venire a prendere
fever febbre f
few, a few pochi, alcuni
fiancé, fiancée fidanzato/a m/f
field campo m
fight (n) lotta f
fight (vb) lottare
file (folder) filza f
file (tool) lima f
fill riempire
fill in compilare
fill up riempirsi
fillet filetto m
filling (tooth) piombatura
film film m, pellicola f
film processing sviluppare
filter filtro m
filthy sudicio/a
find trovare
fine (n) multa f
finger dito m
finish (vb) finire
fire fuoco m
fire brigade vigili del fuoco
fire exit uscita di sicurezza
fire extinguisher estintore m

first, at first primo/a, all'inizio
first aid pronto soccorso m
first-aid kit cassetta di pronto soccorso
first class di prim' ordine, prima classe
first floor primo piano
first name nome di battesimo
fish pesce m
fishing permit permesso di pesca
fishing rod canna da pesca
fishmonger's pescivendolo m
fit in buona salute
fitting room sala di prova f
fix aggiustare
fizzy frizzante
flag bandiera f
flannel flanella f
flash lampo m
flashlight pila f
flask fiasco m
flat (n) appartamento m
flat battery batteria scarica
flat tyre gomma a terra
flavour sapore m
flaw difetto m
flea pulce f
flight volo m
flip flops gli infradito

flippers pinne f
flood alluvione f
floor pavimento m
floorcloth straccio per pavimento
florist fioraio m
flour farina f
flower fiore m
flu influenza f
fluent scorrevole, fluente, fluido
fly (n) mosca f
fly (vb) volare
fog nebbia f
folk gente f
follow seguire
food cibo m
food poisoning intossicazione alimentare
food shop drogheria f
foot piede m
football calcio m
football match partita di calcio
footpath sentiero m
for per
forbidden proibito
forehead fronte f
foreign straniero/a
foreigner straniero m, forestiero m
forest foresta f
forget dimenticare
fork forchetta f
form modulo m
formal formale
fortnight quindicina f

fortress fortezza f
fortunately
   fortunatamente
fountain fontana f
four-wheel-drive
   vehicle fuoristrada f,
   veicolo a trazione a
   4 ruote
fox volpe f
fracture frattura f
frame cornice f
France Francia f
free libero/a
freelance indipendente
freeway autostrada f
freezer congelatore m
French francese
French fries patatine
   fritte
Frenchman/woman
   francese m/f
frequent frequente
fresh fresco/a
Friday venerdì
fridge frigo m
fried fritto
friend amico/a m/f
friendly amichevole
frog rana f
from da
front anteriore
frost gelo m
frozen congelato
fruit frutta f
fruit juice succo di frutta
fruit mince miscuglio
   di frutta candita
fry friggere

frying pan padella f
fuel carburante
fuel gauge indicatore
   della benzina
full pieno/a
full board pensione
   completa
fun divertimento m
funeral funerale m
funicular
   funicolare f
funny divertente
fur pelo m
fur coat pelliccia f
furnished stanza
   ammobiliata
furniture mobili mpl
further ulteriore
fuse fusibile m
fuse box scatola dei
   fusibili
future futuro m

G
gallery galleria f
gallon gallone m
game gioco m
garage garage m
garden giardino m
garlic aglio m
gas benzina f
gas cylinder
   cilindro a gas
gas cooker
   cucina a gas
gate cancello m
gay omosessuale

ENGLISH → ITALIAN

ENGLISH → ITALIAN

gay bar bar omosessuale

gear marcia f

gear lever leva del cambio

gearbox cambio di velocità

general (adj) generale

generous generoso/a

Geneva Ginevra f

gents' toilet toilette per uomini

genuine genuino/a

German (adj, n) tedesco/a m/f

German measles rosolia f

get ricevere

get off scendere

get on salire

get up alzarsi

gift regalo m

girl ragazza f

girlfriend amica f, ragazza f

give dare

give back restituire

glacier ghiacciaio m

glad contento/a

glass bicchiere m

glasses (spectacles) occhiali

gloves guanti m

glue colla f

go andare

go away andarsene

go back ritornare

goat capra f

God Dio m

goggles occhiali di protezione

gold oro m

golf club (place) circolo m del golf

golf club (stick) mazza da golf

golf course campo di golf

good buono/a

good afternoon, good day buon giorno

good evening buona sera

Good Friday Venerdì Santo

Good luck! Buona fortuna!

good morning buon giorno

good night buonanotte

goodbye arrivederci

goose oca f

gothic gotico/a

government governo m

gradually gradualmente

gram grammo m

grammar grammatica f

grand grandioso/a

granddaughter, grandson nipote m/f

grandfather nonno m

grandmother nonna f

grandparents nonni

grape uva

grass erba f

grate (vb) grattugiare
grateful grato/a
gravy sugo di carne
greasy untuoso/a, grasso/a, oleoso/a
great grande
Great Britain Gran Bretagna f
Greece Grecia f
Greek (adj, n) greco m
green verde
greengrocer fruttivendolo m
greeting saluto m
grey grigio/a
grilled alla griglia
ground terra f, suolo m
ground floor pianterreno m
group gruppo m
guarantee garanzia f
guard guardia f
guest ospite m/f
guesthouse pensione f
guide (n) guida f
guide book guida turistica
guided tour escursione con guida
guitar chitarra f
gun pistola f
gym palestra f

H
hail grandine f
hair capelli m
hairbrush spazzola per capelli
haircut taglio di capelli
hairdresser parrucchiere/a m/f
hairdryer asciugacapelli
half metà f
hall sala f
ham prosciutto m
hamburger hamburger
hammer martello m
hand mano f
hand luggage bagaglio a mano
handbag borsa f
handbrake freno a mano
handicapped handicappato/a
handkerchief fazzoletto m
handle maniglia f
handmade fatto a mano
handsome bello
hang-gliding fare deltaplano m
hang up (telephone) riagganciare
hanger attaccapanni
hangover postumi di una sbornia
happen succedere
happy felice
Happy New Year! Buon Anno Nuovo!
harbour porto m
hard duro/a
hard disk disco rigido
hardly appena

hardware shop
  negozio di ferramenta f
hare lepre f
harvest raccolta f
hat cappello m
have avere
hay fever raffreddore
  da fieno
hazelnuts nocciole f
he lui
head testa f, capo m
headache mal di testa
headlights fari mpl
headphones cuffie fpl
health food shop
  negozio di macrobiotica
healthy sano/a, in buona
  salute
hear sentire
hearing aid
  apparecchio acustico
heart cuore m
heart attack infarto
heartburn pirosi
heat calore m
heater termosifone,
  stufa
heating riscaldamento
heavy pesante
heel (foot) tallone m
heel (shoe) tacco m
height altezza f
helicopter elicottero m
helmet casco m
Help! Aiuto!
help (vb) aiutare
hem orlo m
her lei

herbal tea tisana f
herbs erbe f
here qui, qua
hernia ernia f
hide nascondere
high alto/a
high blood pressure
  pressione alta del
  sangue
high chair seggiolone m
high tide alta marea
him lui
hip fianco m
hip replacement
  sostituto di fianco
hire affittare
hire car macchina a
  noleggio
his il suo
historic storico/a
history storia f
hit colpo m
hitchhike fare l'autostop
hold (vb) tenere
hole buco m
holiday vacanza f
holidays vacanze
holy santo/a
home casa f
homesickness
  nostalgia di casa
honest onesto/a
honey miele m
honeymoon
  luna di miele
hood (of car) cofano m
hood (of garment)
  cappuccio m

hope (n) speranza f
hope (vb) sperare
hopefully con speranza
horn (animal) corno m
horn (car) tromba f,
   clacson m
horse cavallo m
horse racing corse di
   cavalli
horse riding
   equitazione (del cavallo)
hose pipe tubo flessibile
hospital ospedale m
hospitality ospitalità f
hostel ostello m
hot caldo/a
hot spring
   sorgente calda
hot-water bottle borsa
   per acqua calda
hour ora f
hourly ogni ora
house casa f
house wine vino di casa
housework lavoro
   domestico
hovercraft hovercraft m
How? Come?
How are you?
   Come stai ?
How do you do?
   Molto lieto!
How many? Quanti?
**How much do I owe
   you?** Quanto le devo?
How much is it?
   Quanto costa questo?
humid umido/a

humour umorismo m
Hungarian (adj, n)
   ungherese m/f
Hungary Ungheria f
hungry: I am hungry
   ho fame
hunt (n) caccia f
hunt (vb) cacciare
hunting permit
   permesso per caccia
hurry (n) fretta f
hurry (vb) affrettare
hurt, it hurts far male,
   mi fa male
husband marito m
hydrofoil aliscafo m
hypodermic needle
   ago ipodermico

I
I io
ice ghiaccio m
ice cream gelato m
ice rink pista di
   pattinaggio
ice skates pattini da
   ghiaccio
iced coffee caffè
   ghiacciato
idea idea f
identity card
   carta d'identità
if se
ignition accensione f
ignition key chiave
   dell'accensione
ill malato/a
illness malattia f

ENGLISH → ITALIAN

immediately immediatamente
important importante
impossible impossibile
improve migliorare
in in, nel
inch pollice m
included incluso
inconvenient scomodo/a
incredible incredibile
Indian (adj, n) indiano/a m/f
indicator freccia f
indigestion indigestione f
indoor pool piscina coperta, piscina interna
indoors dentro
infection infenzione f
infectious infettivo/a
inflammation infiammazione f
informal informale
information informazioni f
ingredients ingredienti mpl
injection iniezione f
injured ferito/a
injury ferita f
ink inchiostro m
in-laws parenti acquisiti
inn locanda f
inner tube camera d'aria f
insect insetto m

insect bite puntura di insetto m
insect repellent insettifugo m
inside interno
insist insistere
insomnia insonnia f
instant coffee caffè solubile
instead invece
insulin insulina f
insurance assicurazione f
intelligent intelligente
interesting interessante
international internazionale
interpreter interprete m/f
intersection intersezione f
interval intervallo m
into dentro a
introduce presentare
invitation invito m
invite invitare
invoice fattura f
Ireland Irlanda f
Irish irlandese
Irishman/woman irlandese m/f
iron ferro da stiro
ironing board asse da stiro
ironmonger's negozio di ferramenta
is è
island isola f

it lo m, la f
Italian (adj, n)
  italiano/a m/f
Italy Italia f
itch (n) prurito m

J
jack cricco m
jacket giacca f
jam marmellata f
jammed congestionato
janitor portinaio/a m/f
January gennaio m
jar barattolo m
jaundice itterizia f
jaw mascella f
jealous geloso/a
jellyfish medusa f
jersey maglia f
Jew ebreo m
jeweller's gioielleria f
jewellery gioielli m
Jewish ebraico/a
job lavoro m
jog fare jogging
join unire
joint giuntura f
joke scherzo m
journey viaggio m
joy gioia f
jug brocca f
judge (n) giudice
judge (vb) giudicare
juice succo m
July luglio m
jump saltare
jump leads cavi con
  morsetti

jumper golf m
junction giunzione m,
  congiungimento m,
  raccordo m
June giugno m
just (fair) giusto/a
just (only) proprio,
  appena

K
keep tenere
Keep the change!
  Tenga il resto!
kettle bollitore (per
  l'acqua)
key chiave f
key ring portachiavi m
kick (n) calcio m
kick (vb) prendere a
  calci
kidney rene m
kill uccidere
kilo, kilogram chilo m,
  chilogrammo m
kilometre chilometro m
kind (adj) gentile
kind (n) sorta f
king re m
kiosk chiosco m
kiss (n) bacio m
kiss (vb) baciare
kitchen cucina f
kitchenette cucinino m
knee ginocchio m
knickers mutandine f
knife coltello m
knit lavorare a maglia
knit wear maglieria f

ENGLISH → ITALIAN

knitting needle ferro da calza
knock bussare
knock down investire
knock over rovesciare
know sapere

L
label etichetta f
lace (fabric) pizzo m
lace (for shoe) laccio m
ladder scala f
ladies' toilet toilette per donne
ladies' wear l'abbigliamento da donna
lady signora f
lager birra f
lake lago m
Lake Garda Lago di Garda
Lake Maggiore Lago Maggiore
lamb agnello m
lamp lampada f
land terra f
landlady proprietaria f
landlord proprietario m
landslide frana f
lane sentiero m
language lingua f
language course corso di lingua
large grande
last ultimo/a

last night ieri sera, ieri notte
last week scorsa settimana
late ritardo/a, tardi
later più tardi
Latvia Lettonia f
laugh (n) risata f
laugh (vb) ridere
launderette, laundromat lavanderia f
laundry bucato m
lavatory gabinetto m
law legge f
lawyer avvocato m
laxative lassativo m
lazy pigro/a
lead (n) piombo m
lead (vb) condurre
lead-free senza piombo
leaf foglia f
leaflet volantino m
leak (n) perdita f
leak (vb) perdere
learn imparare
lease (n) contratto d'affitto m
lease (vb) affittare
leather pelle f
leave lasciare
leek porro m
left sinistra
left-handed mancino/a
leg gamba f
lemon limone m
lemonade limonata f
lend prestare

lens lente f
lentils lenticchie f
lesbian lesbica f
less meno
lesson lezione f
let (allow) permettere
let off (oneself)
  lasciarsi andare
letter lettera f
letterbox buca per le
  lettere
lettuce lattuga f
level crossing
  passaggio a livello
lever leva f
library biblioteca f
licence licenza f,
  patente f (for driving)
lid coperchio m
lie (n, untruth) bugia f
lie (vb, fib) mentire
lie (vb, recline) giacere
lie down sdraiarsi
life vita f
life belt salvagente m
life guard bagnino m
life insurance
  assicurazione sulla vita
life jacket giubbotto
  di salvataggio
lift (n, elevator)
  ascensore m
lift (vb) sollevare
light (adj, not dark)
  chiaro/a
light (adj, not heavy)
  leggero/a
light (n) luce f

light bulb lampadina f
lightning lampo m
like (adj) simile
like (prep) come, da
like (vb) piacere
lime calce f
linen lino m
lingerie biancheria f
lion leone m
lipstick rossetto m
liqueur liquore
list lista f
listen ascoltare
Lithuania Lituania f
litre litro m
litter (n) rifiuti mpl
litter (vb) disseminare
little piccolo/a, poco/a
live vivere
lively vivace
liver fegato m
living room
  soggiorno m
loaf pagnotta f
lobby atrio m
lobster aragosta f
local locale
lock (n) serratura f
lock (vb) chiudere
lock in chiudere dentro
lock out chiudere fuori
locker armadietto m
lollipop lecca-lecca
long (adj) lungo/a
long (adv) lungamente
long-distance call
  chiamata interurbana
look after badare

ENGLISH → ITALIAN

look at guardare
look for cercare
look forward to essere
 impaziente di
loose libero/a
lorry camion m
lose perdere
lost perduto/a
lost property oggetti
 smarriti
lot molto
loud forte
lounge salotto m
love (n) amore m
love (vb) amare
lovely bello/a
low basso/a
low fat magro
low tide bassa marea
luck fortuna f
lucky fortunato/a
luggage bagaglio m
luggage rack
 portabagagli m
luggage tag etichetta
 per bagagli
luggage trolley carello
 portabagagli
lump bernoccolo m
lunch pranzo m
lung polmone m
Luxembourg
 Lussenburgo
luxury lusso m

M
machine macchina f
mad pazzo/a

made fatto/a
magazine rivista f
maggot verme m
magnet magnete m
magnifying glass lente
 d'ingrandimento
maid cameriera f
maiden name
 cognome da nubile
mail (n) posta f
mail (vb) impostare
main principale
main course
 portata principale
main post office
 l'ufficio postale
 principale
main road strada
 principale
mains switch
 interruttore principale
make fare
male maschile
man uomo m
man-made fibre
 tessuto sintetico
manager direttore m
manual (adj) manuale
manual (n) manuale m
many molti
map carta geografica f
marble (n, stone)
 marmo m
marble (n, toy)
 pallina f
March marzo m
market mercato m

marmalade marmellata
d'arance
married sposato/a
marsh palude f
mascara mascara m
mashed potatoes
purè di patate
mass (volume) massa
f
Mass (rel) Messa f
mast albero m
match (n, game)
incontro m
matches (for lighting)
fiammiferi **mpl**
material stoffa f
matter faccenda f
matter: It doesn't
matter Non importa
matter: What's the
matter? Che cosa
c'è?
mattress materasso m
May maggio m
may (vb, be able to)
potere
maybe forse
mayonnaise maionese f
me mi
meal pasto m
mean (adj, nasty)
meschino/a
mean (vb, intend)
intendere
measles morbillo m
measure (n) misura f
measure (vb) misurare
meat carne f

mechanic
meccanico m
medical insurance
assicurazione sanitaria
medicine medicina f
medieval medievale
Mediterranean
mediterraneo
medium medio/a
medium dry (wine)
vino amabile
medium rare (meat)
non troppo cotto/a
medium sized di taglia
media
meet incontrare
meeting incontro m
melon melone m
melt sciogliere
men uomini m
mend riparare
meningitis meningite f
menswear
l'abbigliamento da uomo
mention (n) menzione f
mention (vb)
menzionare
menu menu m
meringue meringa f
message messaggio m
metal metallo m
meter contatore m
metre metro m
metro la metropolitana
microwave forno a
microonde
midday mezzogiorno m
middle di mezzo m

ENGLISH → ITALIAN

115

ENGLISH → ITALIAN

midnight mezzanotte
might potere
migraine emicrania f
mile miglio m
milk latte m
mind (n) mente f,
  intelligenza f
mind (vb, take care)
  badare
mineral water acqua
  minerale
minister (church)
  pastore m
minister (politics)
  ministro m
mint menta f
minute (adj, size)
  minuto/a
minute (n, time)
  minuto m
mirror specchio m
Miss signorina
miss (vb) mancare
missing mancante
mist foschia f
mistake sbaglio m
misunderstanding
  malinteso m
mix mescolare
mix up confondere
mobile phone telefono
  cellulare
moisturizer crema
  idratante
moment momento m
monastery
  monastero m
Monday lunedì m

money soldi m
money belt cintura
  portasoldi
money order vaglia
  postale
month mese m
monthly mensile
monument
  monumento m
moon luna f
mooring ormeggio m
more più
morning mattina f
mosque moschea f
mosquito zanzara f
most la maggior parte di
mostly per lo più
moth falena f
mother madre f
mother-in-law
  suocera f
motor motore m
motorbike
  motocicletta f
motorboat
  motoscafo m
motorway autostrada f
mountain montagna f
mountain rescue
  soccorso alpino
mountaineering
  alpinismo m
mouse topo m
moustache baffi m
mouth bocca f
mouth ulcer stomatite
mouthwash colluttorio
  m, acqua dentifricia f

move muovere
Mr Signor m
Mrs/Ms Signora f,
  Signorina f
much molto/a
mud fango m
mug boccale m
mugged aggredito/a
  e derubato/a
mumps orecchioni mpl
Munich Monaco
  di Baviera
muscle muscolo m
museum museo m
mushroom fungo m
musician musicista m/f
Muslim musulmano m
mussels cozze fpl
must dovere
mustard senape f
mutton carne di
  montone
my il mio m, la mia f
myself io stesso

N
nail unghia f
nail brush spazzolino
  da unghie m
nail file limetta da
  unghie f
nail polish/varnish
  smalto per unghie m
nail polish remover
  acetone
nail scissors forbicine
  da unghie
name nome m

nanny bambinaia f
napkin tovagliolo m
nappy pannolino m
narrow stretto/a
nasty cattivo/a
national nazionale
nationality nazionalità f
natural naturale
nature natura f
nature reserve riserva
  naturale f
nausea nausea f
navy marina f
navy blue blu marino m
near vicino
nearby vicino
nearly quasi
necessary necessario/a
neck collo m
necklace collana f
need (n) bisogno m
need (vb) bisognare
needle ago m
negative negativo/a
neighbour vicino/a m/f
neither ... nor nè ... nè
nephew nipote m
nest nido m
net rete f
Netherlands
  Paesi Bassi
never mai
new nuovo/a
New Year Anno Nuovo
New Year's Eve
  Vigilia di Capodanno
New Zealand Nuova
  Zelanda f

ENGLISH → ITALIAN

New Zealander
  Neozelandese m/f
news notizie fpl
news stand edicola f
newspaper giornale m
next prossimo/a
next week la prossima
  settimana
nice bello/a
niece nipote f
night notte f
nightdress camicia da
  notte
no no
nobody nessuno m
noise rumore m
noisy rumoroso/a
non-alcoholic
  analcolico m
non-smoking
  non fumatori
none niente
noon mezzogiorno
north nord m
North Sea Mare del
  Nord m
Northern Ireland
  Irlanda del Nord f
Norway Norvegia f
Norwegian
  norvegese m/f
nose naso m
not non
note nota f
notebook/paper
  taccuino m, carta
  da lettere
nothing niente, nulla

nothing else nient'altro
notice board tabellone
novel romanzo m
November novembre m
now adesso
nudist beach spiaggia
  per nudisti
number numero m
number plate targa f
nurse, male nurse
  infermiera, infermiere
nursery stanza dei
  bambini
nursery school scuola
  materna f
nursery slope pista per
  principianti
nut noce f
nut (for bolt) dado m

O
oak quercia f
oar remo m
oats avena f
obtain ottenere
occasionally ogni tanto
occupation
  occupazione f
occupied (e.g. toilet)
  occupato/a
ocean oceano m
October ottobre m
odd (of numbers)
  dispari
odd (strange) strano/a
of di
off spento
office ufficio m

often spesso

oil olio m

ointment pomata f

okay va bene

old vecchio/a

old-age pensioner pensionato m

old-fashioned antiquato/a

olive oliva f

olive oil olio di oliva

omelette omelette f, frittata f

on su, sopra

once una volta f

one uno, una

one-way street senso unico

onion cipolla f

only solo

open aperto/a

open ticket biglietto aperto m

opening times orario d'apertura

opera opera f

operation operazione f

operator (phone) centralinista m/f

opposite opposto/a

optician ottico m

or o

orange arancia f

orange juice succo d'arancia

orchestra orchestra f

order (n) ordine m

order (vb) ordinare

organic (vegetables) organico/a

other altro/a

otherwise altrimenti

our nostro/a

out fuori

out of order guasto

outdoors all'aperto

outside esterno m

oven forno m

ovenproof pirofilo/ resistente al calore

over sopra

over here qui

over there là

overcharged far pagare più del dovuto

overcoat cappotto m

overdone stracotto

overheat surriscaldare

overnight per la notte

overtake sorpassare

owe dovere

owl gufo m

owner proprietario/a m/f

P

pacemaker pacemaker m

pack (of cards) mazzo m

package pacco m

package holiday vacanza organizzata

packet pacchetto m

padlock lucchetto m

page pagina f

paid pagato

ENGLISH → ITALIAN

ENGLISH → ITALIAN

pail secchio m
pain dolore m
painful doloroso/a
painkiller analgesico m
paint (n) pittura f
paint (vb) pitturare
painting (picture)
　quadro m
pair paio m
palace palazzo m
pale pallido/a
pan padella f
pancake frittella f
panties mutandine f
pants mutande f
pantyhose collant m
paper carta f
paper napkins
　tovaglioli di carta
parcel pacco m
Pardon? Scusi?
parents genitori m
parents-in-law
　suoceri m
park (n) parco m
park (vb) parcheggiare
parking disc disco
　parcheggio m
parking meter
　parchimetro m
parking ticket multa
　per divieto di sosta
part parte f
partner (business)
　socio m
partner (companion)
　compagno/a m/f

party (celebration)
　festa f
party (political)
　partito m
pass (n) passo m
pass (vb) passare
pass control
　controllo m
passenger
　passeggero m
passport
　passaporto m
past passato/a
pastry pasta f
path sentiero m
patient (adj) paziente
patient (n) paziente m/f
pattern disegno m
pavement
　marciapiede m
pay pagare
payment
　pagamento m
payphone telefono
　pubblico m
pea pisello m
peach pesca f
peak picco m
peak rate tariffa
　massima f
peanut arachide m
pear pera f
pearl perla f
peculiar strano/a
pedal pedale m
pedestrian pedone m
pedestrian crossing
　passaggio pedonale

peel (n) buccia f
peel (vb) sbucciare
peg piolo m
pen penna f
pencil matita f
penfriend amico di penna
peninsula penisola f
pensioner pensionato m
people persone f
pepper pepe m
per per
perfect perfetto/a
performance esecuzione f
perfume profumo m
perhaps forse
period periodo m
perm permanente
permit (n) permesso m
permit (vb) permettere
person persona f
pet animale domestico m
petrol benzina f
petrol can latta per benzina f
petrol station stazione di servizio
pharmacy farmacia f
phone telefono m
phone book elenco telefonico m
phone booth cabina telefonica f
phone call telefonata f

phone card scheda telefonica f
phone number numero telefonico m
photo, to take a photo foto f, fare una foto
photocopy fotocopia f
phrase book libro di fraseologia
piano piano m
pickpocket borsaiolo m
picnic picnic m
picture disegno m
picture frame cornice f
pie torta f
piece pezzo m
pig maiale m
pill pillola f
pillow guanciale m
pillowcase federa f
pilot pilota f
pin spillo m
pineapple ananas m
pink rosa
pipe pipa f
pity, It's a pity peccato, È un peccato
place (n) posto m
place (vb) posare, porre
plain semplice
plait treccia f
plane aeroplano m
plant (n) pianta f
plant (vb) piantare
plaster gesso m
plastic plastica f

ENGLISH → ITALIAN

plastic bag sacchetto di plastica
plate piatto m
platform binario m
play (n, game) gioco m
play (n, theatre) dramma m
play (vb) giocare
playground cortile m
please per favore
pleased lieto/a
Pleased to meet you! Molto lieto/piacere!
plenty abbondanza f
pliers pinze f
plug (bath) tappo m
plug (elec) spina f
plum prugna f
plumber idraulico m
p.m. (after noon) del pomeriggio
poached egg uovo in camicia
pocket tasca f
point (n) punto m
point (vb) indicare
points (car) puntine f
poison veleno m
poisonous velenoso/a
Poland Polonia f
police polizia f
police station commissariato m
policeman poliziotto m
policewoman (donna) poliziotta
Polish polacco m

polish (n) lucido m
polish (vb) lucidare
polite cortese
polluted inquinato
pool pozza f
poor (impoverished) povero/a
poor (quality) scandente
poppy papavero m
popular popolare
population popolazione
pork carne di maiale
port (harbour) porto m
port (wine) Vino di Oporto m
porter portiere m
portion porzione f
portrait ritratto m
Portugal Portogallo m
Portuguese (adj, n) portoghese m/f
posh danaroso/a
possible possibile
post (n) posta f
post (vb) impostare
post box cassetta delle lettere
post office ufficio postale
postage affrancatura f
postage stamp francobollo m
postal code codice postale
postcard cartolina f
poster manifesto m

postman/woman
postino/a **m/f**
postpone rimandare
potato patata **f**
pothole buca **f**
pottery ceramica **f**
pound (money)
sterlina **f**
pound (weight) libbra **f**
pour versare
powder polvere **f**
powdered milk latte in
polvere
power cut interruzione
di corrente
practice pratica **f**
practise praticare
pram carrozzella **f**
prawn gambero **m**
pray pregare
prefer preferire
pregnant incinta
prescription ricetta **f**
present (adj) presente
present (n) regalo **m**
present (vb) pre-
sentare
pressure pressione **f**
pretty carino/a
price prezzo **m**
priest prete **m**
Prime Minister
Primo Ministro **m**
print (n) stampa **f**
print (vb) stampare
printed matter
stampe
prison prigione **f**

private privato/a
prize premio **m**
probably probabilmente
problem problema **m**
programme, program
programma **m**
prohibited vietato
promise promessa **f**
pronounce pronunciare
properly correttamente
Protestant protestante
public pubblico/a
public holiday festa
nazionale
pudding dolce **m**
pull tirare
pullover maglione **m**
pump (n) pompa **f**
pump (vb) pompare
puncture foratura **f**
puppet show
spettacolo burattini **m**
purple viola
purse borsellino **m**
push spingere
pushchair
passeggino **m**
put mettere
put up (guest) ospitare
pyjamas pigiama **f**

Q
quality qualità **f**
quantity quantità **f**
quarantine
quarantena **f**
quarrel (n) lite **f**
quarrel (vb) litigare

ENGLISH → ITALIAN

ENGLISH → ITALIAN

quarter quarto m
quay banchina f
queen regina f
question (n)
　domanda f
question (vb)
　domandare
queue fila f
quickly fretta, presto
quiet tranquillo/a
quilt trapunta f
quite completamente

R
rabbit coniglio m
rabies rabbia f
race (people) razza f
race (sport) corsa f
race course
　ippodromo m
racket racchetta f
radiator radiatore m
radio radio f
radish ravanello m
rag straccio m
railway ferrovia f
railway station
　stazione ferroviaria
rain pioggia f
raincoat
　impermeabile m
raisin uva passa
rake rastrello m
rape (n) violazione f
rape (vb) violentare
rare raro/a
rash eruzione f
raspberry lampone m

rat topo m
rate (of exchange)
　tasso m
raw crudo/a
razor rasoio m
razor blades lamette
　da barba
read leggere
ready pronto
real vero/a
realize realizzare
really davvero
rear-view mirror
　specchietto retrovisore
reasonable ragionevole
receipt ricevuta f
receiver ricevitore m
recently recentemente
reception ricezione f
receptionist impiegato
　ricezione
recharge ricaricare
recipe ricetta f
recognize riconoscere
recommend
　raccomandare
record (n) documento m
record (vb) registrare
red rosso
red wine vino rosso m
redcurrants
　mirtilli rossi
reduce ridurre
reduction riduzione f
refund (n) rimborso m
refund (vb) rimborsare
refuse (n) immondizia f
refuse (vb) rifiutare

region regione f
register (n) registro m
register (vb) registrare
registered mail posta
   raccomandata
registration form
   modulo registrazione
registration number
   targa f
relative, relation
   parente m/f
remain restare
remember ricordare
rent (n) affitto m
rent (vb) affittare
repair (n) riparazione f
repair (vb) riparare
repeat ripetere
reply (n) risposta f
reply (vb) rispondere
report (n) rapporto m
report (vb) rapportare
request (n) richiesta f
request (vb) richiedere
require richiedere
rescue (n)
   salvamento m
rescue (vb) salvare
reservation (seats)
   prenotazione f
reserve riserva f
resident residente m/f
resort luogo di
   villeggiatura
rest (n, relaxation)
   riposo m
rest (n, remainder)
   resto m

rest (vb) riposare
retired andare in
   pensione
return (n) ritorno m
return (vb) ritornare
return ticket biglietto di
   andata e ritorno
reverse invertire
reverse-charge call
   chiamata a carico del
   destinatario
reverse gear marcia
   indietro
revolting rivoltante
rheumatism
   reumatismo m
rib costola f
ribbon nastro m
rice riso m
rich ricco/a
ridiculous ridicolo/a
ride (n) cavalcata f
ride (vb) cavalcare
right (correct)
   corretto/a
right (direction)
   destro/a
right (fair) giusto/a
right-hand drive guida
   a destra
ring (n) anello m
ring (vb) suonare
ring road
   circonvallazione f
ripe maturo/a
rip-off frode f
river fiume m
road strada f

road accident
  incidente
road map
  carta stradale **f**
road sign cartello/
  segnale stradale **m**
roadworks lavori
  stradali **m**
rock roccia **f**
roll panino **m**
roof tetto **m**
roof-rack
  portabagagli **m**
room camera **f**
rope corda **f**
rose rosa **f**
rotten marcio/a
rough ruvido/a
roughly pressappoco
round rotondo/a
roundabout giostra **f**
row (n, queue) fila **f**
row (n, noise)
  rumore **m**
row (vb, boat) remare
royal reale
rubber gomma **f**
rubbish immondizia **f**
rubella rosolia **f**
rudder timone **m**
rug tappeto **m**
ruin (n) rovina **f**
ruin (vb) rovinare
ruler (for measuring)
  regolo **m**
ruler (sovereign)
  sovrano **m**
rum rum **m**

run correre
rush (n) fretta **f**
rush (vb) affrettare
rusty arrugginito/a
rye bread pane di
  segale **f**

S
sad triste
saddle sella **f**
safe sicuro/a
safety belt cintura di
  sicurezza
safety pin spillo di
  sicurezza **m**
sail (n) vela **f**
sail (vb) navigare
sailing navigazione **f**
salad insalata **f**
salad dressing
  condimento per insalata
sale vendita **f**
sales representative
  rappresentante **m**
salesperson
  venditore **m**
salmon salmone **m**
salt sale **m**
same stesso/a
sand sabbia **f**
sandals sandali **mpl**
sandwich tramezzino **m**
sanitary pads
  assorbenti igienici **m**
Saturday sabato
sauce salsa **f**
saucer piattino **m**
sausage salsiccia **f**

save salvare
savoury salato/a, saporito
say dire
scale bilancia **f**
scarf sciarpa **f**
scenery scenario **m**
school scuola **f**
scissors forbici **f**
Scot scozzese **m/f**
Scotland Scozia **f**
Scottish scozzese
scrambled eggs uova strapazzate
scratch (n) graffio **m**
scratch (vb) graffiare
screen schermo **m**
screw (n) vite **f**
screw (vb) avvitare
screwdriver cacciavite **m**
scrubbing brush spazzolino per le unghie
scuba diving immersioni subacquee
sea mare **m**
seagull gabbiano **m**
seasickness mal di mare
seaside spiaggia **f**
seaweed alga marina **f**
season stagione **f**
season ticket abbonamento **m**
seasoning condimento **m**
seat sedia **f**
seat belt cintura di

sicurezza **f**
secluded appartato/a
second (adj, number) secondo/a
second (n, of time) secondo **m**
second class seconda classe
second hand (of clock) lancetta dei secondi **f**
second-hand (used) usato, di seconda
secretary segretario **m**
security guard guardia di sicurezza
see vedere
self-catering in un appartamento attrezza to di cucina
self-employed che lavora in proprio
self-service self service
sell vendere
sell-by date data di scadenza **f**
send mandare
senior citizen anziano **m**
sentence (grammar) frase **f**
sentence (law) sentenza **f**
separate (adj) separato/a
separate (vb) separare

September
  settembre **m**
septic settico/a
septic tank fossa
  biologica/settica **f**
serious serio/a
service servizio **m**
service charge
  servizio **m**
set menu menù fisso
several parecchi
sew cucire
sex (gender) sesso **m**
sex (intercourse)
  coito **m**
shade ombra **f**
shake scuotere
shallow poco profondo
shame vergogna **f**
shampoo and set
  shampoo e messa
  in piega
share (n) parte **f**
share (vb) dividere
sharp tagliente
shave radere
she lei **f**
sheep pecora **f**
sheet lenzuolo **m**
shelf scaffale **m**
shellfish frutti di mare
sheltered ritirato/a
shine splendere
shingle ghiaia **f**
shingles fuochi di
  Sant'Antonio
ship nave **f**
shirt camicia **f**

shock absorber
  ammortizzatore **m**
shoe scarpa **f**
shoe laces
  lacci da scarpa
shop negozio **m**
shop assistant
  commesso **m**
shop window vetrina **f**
shopping centre
  centro commerciale **m**
shore riva **f**
short corto/a
short-cut scorciatoia **f**
short-sighted miope
shorts calzoncini corti
should dovere
shoulder spalla **f**
shout (n) grido **m**
shout (vb) gridare
show (n) mostra **f**
show (vb) mostrare
shower doccia **f**
shrimps gamberetti **mpl**
shrink restringersi
shut chiudere
shutter serranda **f**
shy timido/a
**sick, I'm going to be
  sick!** ammalato/a,
  Mi sento male!/Ho voglia
  di vomitare!
side lato **m**
side dish contorno **m**
sidewalk
  marciapiede **m**
sieve setaccio **m**
sight vista **f**

sightseeing andare a
visitare posti
sign (n) segno m
sign (vb) firmare
signal segnale m
signature firma f
signpost segnale
stradale f
silence silenzio m
silk seta f
silly sciocco/a
silver argento m
similar simile
simple semplice
sing cantare
singer cantante m/f
single solo
single bed letto singolo
single room
camera singola
single ticket biglietto
di andata
sink lavandino m
sister sorella f
sister-in-law
cognata f
sit sedere
size misura f
skate (n) pattino m
skate (vb) pattinare
skating rink pista di
pattinaggio
ski (n) sci m
ski (vb) sciare
ski boot scarponi da sci
ski jump trampolino
per sci
ski slope pista per sci

skin pelle f
skirt gonna f
sky cielo m
sledge slitta f
sleep dormire
sleeping bag
sacco a pelo m
sleeping car
vagone letto
sleeping pill
sonnifero m
sleepy assonnato/a
slice (n) fetta f
slice (vb) affettare
slide (n) scivolo m
slide (vb) scivolare
slip (n) scivolata f
slip (vb) scivolare
slippers pantofole f
slippery scivoloso
slow lento/a
slowly lentamente
small piccolo/a
smell (n) odore m
smell (vb) odorare
smile (n) sorriso m
smile (vb) sorridere
smoke (n) fumo m
smoke (vb) fumare
smoked salmon
salmone affumicato
snack spuntino m
snake serpente m
sneeze (n) starnuto m
sneeze (vb) starnutire
snore russare
snorkel respiratore m

snow, it is snowing neve f, nevica
soaking solution soluzione per lenti a contatto
soap sapone m
soap powder detersivo in polvere
sober sobrio/a
socket presa di corrente
socks calzini m
soda soda f
soft morbido/a
soft drink bibita analcolica f
sole (fish) sogliola f
sole (foot) pianta f
sole (shoe) suola f
soluble solubile
some alcuni, qualche
someone, somebody qualcuno m
something qualcosa
sometimes qualche volta
somewhere da qualche parte
son figlio m
son-in-law genero m
song canzone f
soon presto
sore, it's sore dolorante, fa male
sore throat mal di gola
Sorry! Mi dispiace!
sort (n) specie f
sort (vb) classificare
soup minestra f

sour agro/a
south sud m
South Africa Sudafrica f
South African (adj, n) sudafricano/a m/f
souvenir ricordo souvenir m
spa stazione termale f
spade vanga f
Spain Spagna f
Spaniard spagnolo/a m/f
Spanish spagnoli/e m/f
spanner chiave inglese
spare part pezzo di ricambio
spare tyre/wheel ruota di scorta
spark plug candela f
sparkling frizzante
speak parlare
speciality specialità
spectacles occhiali m
speed velocità f
speed limit limite di velocità
speedometer tachimetro m
spell (n, magic) incantesimo m
spell (vb, grammar) compitare
spend spendere
spice spezia f
spider ragno m
spill rovesciare
spinach spinaci m
spin-dryer centrifuga f

spine spina dorsale f
spirits spirito m
splinter scheggia f
spoil rovinare
spoke raggio m
sponge spugna f
spoon cucchiaio m
sprain (vb) slogare
spring (metal) molla f
spring (season)
   primavera f
square (adj) quadra-
to/a
square (n) piazza f
stadium stadio m
stain macchia f
stairs scale f
stale stantio/a
stalls bancarelle f
stamp francobollo m
staple fermare con
   una graffa
star (film) divo/a m/f
star (sky) stella f
start cominciare
starter (car)
   avviatore m
starter (meal)
   antipasto m
station stazione f
stationer's cartoleria f
statue statua f
stay rimanere
steal rubare
steam vapore m
steep ripido/a
steer sterzare
steering wheel volante

step gradino m
stepfather patrigno m
stepmother matrigna f
stew stufato m
stick (n) bastone m
stick (vb) aderire
sticking plaster
   cerotto m
still ancora
sting (n) puntura f
sting (vb) pungere
stitch punto m
stock scorta f
stocking calza f
stolen rubato
stomach stomaco m
stomachache
   mal di stomaco
stone pietra f
stop (n) fermata f
stop (vb) fermare
stop over pernottare
store magazzino m
storey piano m
storm tempesta f
straight diritto/a
straight on tirare diritto
straightaway
   immediatamente, subito
strange strano/a
stranger estraneo m
strap cinghia f
straw paglia f
strawberry fragola f
stream ruscello m
street strada f
street map
   pianta stradale

strike sciopero **m**
string corda **f**
striped a strisce
stroke colpo **m**
strong forte
stuck inceppato
student studente **m**
student discount
  sconto per studenti
stuffed ripieno **m**
stupid stupido/a
subtitle sottotitolo **m**
suburb sobborgo **m**
subway metropolitana **f**
suddenly
  improvvisamente
suede camoscio **m**
sugar zucchero **m**
sugar-free
  senza zucchero
suit vestito **m**
suitcase valigia **f**
summer estate **f**
summit cima **f**
sun sole **m**
sun block crema solare
sunburn scottatura **f**
Sunday domenica **f**
sunglasses
  occhiali da sole
sunny assolato/a
sunrise alba **f**
sunroof tettuccio apribile
sunset tramonto **m**
sunshade parasole **m**
sunshine luce del sole
sunstroke insolazione **f**
suntan oil olio solare

suntanned
  abbronzato/a
supper cena **f**
supplement
  supplemento **m**
sure certo/a, sicuro/a
surfboard tavola da surf
surgery (doctor's rooms) gabinetto
  medico
surgery (procedure)
  chirurgia **f**
surname cognome **m**
surrounded circondato
suspension
  sospensione **f**
swallow inghiottire
swear (an oath)
  giurare
swear (curse)
  bestemmiare
swear word
  parolaccia **f**,
  bestemmia **f**
sweat (n) sudore **m**
sweat (vb) sudare
sweater maglione **m**
Swede svedese **m/f**
Sweden Svezia **f**
Swedish svedese
sweet dolce
swell gonfiare
swelling gonfiore **m**
swim nuotare
swimming costume
  costume da bagno **m**
swing altalena **f**
Swiss svizzero/a **m/f**

Swiss-German
svizzero/a tedesco/a
switch interruttore m
switch off spegnere
switch on accendere
Switzerland Svizzera f
swollen gonfio/a
synagogue sinagoga f

T
table tavolo m
table wine
vino da tavola
tablecloth tovaglia f
tablespoon
cucchiaio (da tavola)
tailor sarto m
take prendere
take-away food piatto
da portar via, fuori,
piatto da asporto
take care badare
talcum powder
talco m
talk parlare
tall alto/a
tampon tampone m
tan abbronzatura f
tangerine mandarino m
tank serbatoio m
tape nastro m
tape measure metro m
tape recorder
registratore m
taste (n) gusto m
taste (vb) assaggiare
tax tassa f
taxi taxi, tassì

taxi driver tassista m/f
taxi rank
posteggio per taxi
tea tè
teabag bustina di tè
teach insegnare
teacher insegnante m/f
team squadra f
teapot teiera f
tear (n) rottura f
tear (vb) rompere
teaspoon
cucchiaino (da tè)
teat tettarella f
teeth denti mpl
telephone telefono m
telephone call
chiamata
television televisione f
tell dire
temperature
temperatura f
temple (anat) tempia f
temple (rel) tempio m
temporary
temporaneo/a
tendon tendine m
tennis tennis m
tennis court
campo da tennis
tennis racket
racchetta da tennis
tent tenda f
tent peg piolo da tenda
terminal terminale
thank ringraziare
that quello, quel
the il, la , lo, i, gli, le

ENGLISH → ITALIAN

theatre teatro m
theft furto m
there là
thermometer termometro m
they loro
thick spesso/a
thief ladro/a m/f
thigh coscia f
thin sottile
thing cosa f
think pensare
third-party insurance assicurazione per terzi
thirsty assetato/a
this questo
this morning stamattina
this way da questa parte
this week questa settimana
thorn spina f
those quelli, quei, quegli
thousand mille m
thread filo m
throat gola f
throat lozenges pastiglie per la gola
through attraverso
throw gettare
thumb pollice m
thunder tuono m
thunderstorm temporale m
Thursday giovedì m
ticket biglietto m
ticket collector controllore m

ticket office biglietteria f
tide marea
tie cravatta f
tight stretto/a
tights collant m
till (cash register) cassa f
till (until) fino a
time ora
timetable orario m
tin barattolo m
tin opener apriscatole
tinfoil stagnola f
tiny minuscolo/a
tip mancia f
tired stanco/a
tissue fazzolettino di carta
to a
today oggi m
toe dito del piede m
together insieme
toilet toilette, gabinetto m
toll pedaggio
toll road strada a pedaggio
tomato pomodoro m
tomato juice succo di pomodoro
tomorrow domani
tomorrow afternoon domani pomeriggio
tomorrow evening domani sera

ENGLISH → ITALIAN

tomorrow morning
domani mattina
tongue lingua f
tonight stasera,
questa sera f
tonsillitis tonsillite f
too anche
tool attrezzo m
toolkit borsa arnesi
tooth dente m
toothache mal di denti
toothbrush
spazzolino da denti
toothpick
stuzzicadente
top tappo m
top floor ultimo piano
topless senza
reggiseno
torch torcia f
torn bucato/a
total totale m
tough duro/a
tour giro m
tour guide guida f
tour operator
operatore turistico m
tow rimorchiare
towel asciugamano m
tower torre f
town città f
town hall municipio m
toy giocattolo m
tracksuit tuta da
ginnastica f
traffic traffico m
traffic jam ingorgo m
traffic light semaforo m

trailer rimorchio m
train treno m
tram tram m
tranquillizer
tranquillante m
translate tradurre
translation
traduzione f
translator
traduttore m
trash spazzatura f
travel viaggiare
travel agent agente di
viaggio
travel documents
documenti di viaggio
travel sickness
mal d'auto, d'aereo,
di nave
traveller's cheque
assegni per viaggiatori
tray vassoio m
tree albero m
trolley carrello m
trouble guaio m
trousers pantaloni m
trout trota f
truck camion m
true vero/a
trunk baule m
try provare
try on provarsi
tuna tonno m
tunnel galleria f
Turk, Turkish (n, adj)
turco/a m/f
Turkey Turchia f
turkey tacchino m

ENGLISH → ITALIAN

turn girare
turn around girarsi
turn off spegnere
turquoise turchese
tweezers pinzette **f**
twice due volte
twin beds
letti gemelli **m**
twins gemelli
type tipo **m**
typical tipico/a
tyre gomma **f**
tyre pressure
pressione delle
gomme

U
ugly brutto/a
U.K. Regno Unito **m**
ulcer ulcera **f**
umbrella ombrello **m**
uncle zio **m**
uncomfortable
scomodo/a
unconscious
privo di sensi
under sotto
underdone al sangue
underground
sottoterra
underpants mutande **f**
understand capire
underwear
biancheria intima **f**
unemployed
disoccupato
United States Stati Uniti
(d'America)

university università **f**
unleaded petrol
benzina senza piombo
unlimited illimitato/a
unlock aprire con la
chiave
unpack
disfare le valigie
unscrew svitare
until fino a
unusual insolito/a
up su
upmarket di qualità
upside down
sottosopra
upstairs al piano di
sopra
urgent urgente
us noi
use usare
useful utile
usual usuale
usually di solito

V
vacancy posto vacante
vacation vacanza **f**
vaccination
vaccinazione **f**
vacuum cleaner
aspirapolvere **m**
valid valido/a
valley valle **f**
valuable di valore
value (n) valore **m**
value (vb) valutare
valve valvola **f**
van furgone **m**

vanilla vaniglia f
VAT imposta sul valore aggiunto
veal vitello m
vegetables verdure f
vegetarian vegetariano m
vehicle veicolo m
vein vena f
vending machine distributore automatico
venereal disease malattia venerea f
very molto/a
vest maglia (della pelle)
vet (veterinarian) veterinario m
via via
Vienna Vienna f
view vista f
village villaggio m
vinegar aceto m
vineyard vigneto m
violet violetto f
virus virus m
visa visto m
visit (n) visita f
visit (vb) visitare
visiting hours orario delle visite
visitor ospite m/f
voice voce f
volcano vulcano m
voltage voltaggio m
vomit vomitare
voucher buono m

W
wage salario m
waist vita f
waistcoat panciotto m
wait aspettare
waiter/waitress cameriere/a m/f
waiting room sala d'aspetto
wake up svegliarsi
wake-up call chiamata di sveglia
Wales Galles m
walk (n) camminata f, passeggiata f
walk (vb) camminare
wall muro m
wallet portafoglio m
walnut noce f
want volere
war guerra f
ward (hospital) padiglione m, corsia f
wardrobe guardaroba f
warehouse magazzino m
warm caldo/a
wash lavare
washbasin lavandino m
washing powder detersivo m
washing-up liquid detersivo per i piatti
wasp vespa f
waste (n) scarto m
waste (vb) sprecare
waste bin pattumiera f
watch (n) orologio m

watch (vb) guardare
watch strap
  cinturino dell'orologio
water acqua f
watermelon anguria f
waterproof
  impermeabile
waterskiing sci
  acquatico
wave onda f
way percorso m
we noi
weak debole
wear portare
weather tempo m
weather forecast
  previsioni del tempo
web ragnatela f
wedding matrimonio m
wedding present
  regalo di nozze
wedding ring fede f
Wednesday
  mercoledì m
week settimana
weekday giorno feriale
weekend fine settimana
weekly settimanale
weigh pesare
weight peso m
weird misterioso/a
welcome benvenuto
well bene
Welsh gallese
were erano
west ovest m
wet bagnato/a
whale balena f

What? Cosa?
What is wrong?
  Che cosa non va?
What's the time?
  Che ora è?
wheel ruota f
wheel clamp
  ceppo bloccaruote
wheelchair
  sedia a rotelle
When? Quando?
Where? Dove?
Which? Quale?
while mentre
whipped cream
  panna montata f
white bianco/a
Who? Chi?
whole tutto/a, intero/a
wholemeal bread
  pane integrale
Whose? Di chi?
Why? Perchè
wide largo/a
widow vedova f
widower vedovo m
wife moglie f
wig parrucca f
win vincere
wind vento m
window finestra f
window seat
  posto al finestrino
windscreen parabrezza
windscreen wiper
  tergicristallo m
windy ventoso/a
wine vino m

ENGLISH → ITALIAN

wine list lista dei vini
winter inverno m
wire filo metallico m
wish (n) desiderio m
wish (vb) desiderare
with con
without senza
witness testimone m/f
wolf lupo m
woman donna f
wood legno m, bosco m
wool lana f
word parola f
work (n) lavoro m
work (vb) lavorare
world mondo m
worried preoccupato/a
worse peggio/a
worth valore m
wrap up avvolgere
wrapping paper carta
   da imballaggio
wrinkles rughe f
wrist polso m
write scrivere
writing paper carta da
   lettere f
wrong sbagliato/a

X
X-ray raggi-X m

Y
yacht panfilo m
year anno m
yellow giallo m
yellow pages
   pagine gialle

yes si
yesterday ieri
yolk tuorlo m
you tu, voi
young giovane
your il tuo, il vostro
youth hostel
   ostello della gioventù

Z
zero zero m
zipper, zip fastener
   cerniera f
zone zona f
zoo zoo m, giardino
   zoologico

ENGLISH → ITALIAN

A
a at, to
a buon mercato
cheap
a più buon mercato
cheaper
a strisce striped
abbaiare bark
(vb, dog)
abbastanza f enough
abbazia f abbey
abbonamento m
season ticket
abbondanza f plenty
abbronzato/a
suntanned
abbronzatura f tan
aborto m abortion
accanto beside
acceleratore m
accelerator
accendere switch on
accendino m
cigarettelighter
accensione f ignition
accento m accent
accettare accept
accettazione bagagli
check in
acchiappare catch
acclamazione f
cheering
accordarsi agree
accordo m
agreement
aceto m vinegar

acetone nail polish
remover
acqua f water
acqua dentifricia f
mouthwash
acqua di colonia f
cologne
acqua minerale
mineral water
acqua potabile
drinking water
adattatore m adapter
aderire stick (vb)
adesso now
adulto m, adulta f
adult
aeroplano m plane,
aeroplane
aeroporto m airport
affare m business
affettare slice (vb)
affittare hire, lease,
rent (vb)
affittare una
macchina car hire
affitto m rent (n)
affollato/a crowded
affrancatura f
postage
affrettare hurry,
rush (vb)
agenda f diary
agente di viaggio
travel agent
agente immobiliare
estate agent
aggiustare fix

aggredito/a e derubato/a mugged
aglio m garlic
agnello m lamb
ago m needle
ago ipodermico hypodermic needle
agricoltore m farmer
agro/a sour
aiutare help (vb)
Aiuto! Help!
al piano di sopra upstairs
al piano di sotto downstairs
al sangue underdone
alba f dawn, sunrise
albero m mast, tree
alcuni a few, some
alga marina f seaweed
alimenti per l'infanzia baby food
aliscafo m hydrofoil
all'aperto outdoors
all'estero abroad
all'inizio at first
alla griglia grilled
allacciare fasten
allacciare la cintura di sicurezza fasten seatbelt
alloggio m accommodation
alloggio prima colazione bed & breakfast

alluvione f flood
alpinismo m mountaineering
alta marea high tide
altalena f swing
altezza f height
alto/a high, tall
altrimenti otherwise
altro/a other
alzarsi get up
amare love (vb)
ambasciata f embassy
ambra f amber
ambulanza f ambulance
amica f friend, girlfriend
amichevole friendly
amico m friend, boyfriend
amico di penna penfriend
ammalato/a sick
ammortizzatore m shock absorber
amore m love (n)
analcolico m non-alcoholic
analgesico m painkiller
ananas m pineapple
anatra f duck
anche also, too
ancora still
andare go
andare a prendere fetch

ITALIAN → ENGLISH

ITALIAN → ENGLISH

andare a visitare posti sightseeing

andare in pensione retired

andarsene go away

anello m ring (n)

anestesia f anaesthetic

angolo m corner

anguilla f eel

anguria f watermelon

animale m animal

animale domestico m pet

anniversario m anniversary

anno m year

Anno Nuovo New Year

annuale annual

anteriore front

antiacido antacid

anticipatamente in advance

anticipo m advance

antico/a ancient

anticoncezionale contraceptive

antimeridiane a.m. (before noon)

antipasto m starter (meal)

antiquato/a old-fashioned

anziano m senior citizen

ape f bee

aperto/a open

apparecchio acustico hearing aid

appartamento m flat (n), apartment

appartato/a secluded

appena hardly, just

appendicite f appendicitis

appuntamento m appointment, date

apribottiglie m bottle opener

aprire con la chiave unlock

apriscatole f can opener, tin opener

aquila f eagle

arachide m peanut

aragosta f lobster

arancia f orange

area f area

argento m silver

aria f air

aria condizionata air conditioning

armadietto m locker

armadio m cupboard

arrabbiato/a angry, cross

arrampicarsi climb

arrestare arrest (vb)

arresto m arrest (n)

arrivederci goodbye

arrivo m arrival

arrugginito/a rusty

arte f art, craft

artista f artist

ascensore m
  lift (n), elevator)
ascesso m abscess
asciugacapelli
  hairdryer
asciugamano m
  towel
**asciugare con
  l'asciugacapelli**
  blow-dry
asciugatore dryer
asciutto/a dry
ascoltare listen
asilo m crèche
aspettare wait, expect
aspettarsi expect
aspirapolvere m
  vacuum cleaner
assaggiare taste (vb)
assalire attack (vb)
asse da stiro
  ironing board
**assegni per
  viaggiatori**
  traveller's cheque
assegno m cheque
assetato/a thirsty
assicurazione f
  insurance
**assicurazione per la
  macchina**
  car insurance
**assicurazione per
  terzi** third-party
  insurance
**assicurazione
  sanitaria** medical
  insurance

**assicurazione sulla
  vita** life insurance
assolato/a sunny
assolutamente
  absolutely
assonnato/a sleepy
assorbenti igienici m
  sanitary pads
atrio m lobby
attaccapanni m
  hanger, coat hanger
attaccare attack (vb)
attacco m attack (n)
attraverso through
attrezzatura f
  equipment
attrezzo m tool
autista f driver
autobus m bus
autolavaggio car wash
autostrada f freeway,
  motorway
autunno m autumn
avena f oats
avere have
avviatore m starter
  (car)
avvisare advise
avvitare screw (vb)
avvocato m lawyer
avvolgere wrap up

B
baciare kiss (vb)
bacio m kiss (n)
badare look after, take
  care, mind (vb)
baffi m moustache

ITALIAN → ENGLISH

ITALIAN → ENGLISH

bagaglio m baggage, luggage
bagaglio a mano hand luggage
bagaglio in eccedenza excess luggage
bagnato/a wet
bagnino m life guard
bagno m bath
baia f bay
balcone m balcony
balena f whale
ballare dance (vb)
bambinaia f nanny
bambino m child
bambola f doll
bancarelle f stalls
banchina f quay
banco m counter, desk
bandiera f flag
bar omosessuale gay bar
barattolo m jar, tin
barba f beard
barbiere m barber
barile m barrel
bassa marea low tide
basso/a low
bastone m stick (n)
batteria scarica flat battery
baule m trunk
Baviera Bavaria
Belgio m Belgium

bello/a beautiful, nice, handsome, lovely
benchè although
benda f bandage
bene well
benvenuto welcome
benzina f petrol, gas
benzina senza piombo lead-free/ unleaded petrol
bere drink (vb)
bernoccolo m lump
berretto m cap
bestemmia f swear word
bestemmiare swear (curse)
bevanda f drink (n)
biancheria f lingerie
biancheria intima f underwear
bianco/a white
bibita analcolica f soft drink
biblioteca f library
bicchiere m glass
bicicletta f bicycle
bidone m bin
biglietteria f ticket office
biglietto m ticket
biglietto aereo m air ticket
biglietto aperto m open ticket
biglietto di andata single ticket

biglietto di andata e ritorno return ticket

biglietto di auguri (di compleanno) (birthday) card

bilancia f scale

binario m platform

binocoli binoculars

biondo/a fair (hair colour)

birra f lager

birra alla spina draught beer

birreria brewery f

biscotto m biscuit, cookie

bisognare need (vb)

bisogno m need (n)

bloccato blocked

blocco di appartamenti m block of flats

blu blue

blu marino m navy blue

bocca f mouth

boccale m mug

bollire boil (vb)

bollitore (per l'acqua) kettle

bombolone doughnut

bordo m edge

borsa f bag, handbag

borsa arnesi toolkit

borsa per acqua calda hot-water bottle

borsa per la spesa carrier bag

borsa termica f cool bag/box

borsaiolo m pickpocket

borsellino m purse

bosco m wood

bottiglia f bottle

bottone m button

braccialetto m bracelet

brezza f breeze

brillante bright

brocca f jug

bronchite f bronchitis

bruciare burn (vb)

bruciatura f burn (n)

brutto/a awful, ugly

Bruxelles Brussels

buca f pothole

buca per le lettere letterbox

bucato/a torn

bucato m laundry

buccia f peel (n)

buco m hole

bugia f lie (n, untruth)

bulbo m bulb (plant)

Buon Anno Nuovo! Happy New Year!

buon giorno good afternoon, good day, good morning

Buona fortuna! Good luck!

ITALIAN → ENGLISH

Buona Pasqua! Happy
Easter!
buona sera good
evening
buonanotte
good night
buono m voucher
buono/a good
burro m butter
bussare knock
bussola f compass
busta f envelope
busta di carta
carrier bag
bustina di tè teabag

C
cabina f cabin
cabina telefonica f
phone booth
cacao m cocoa
caccia f hunt (n)
cacciare hunt (vb)
cacciavite m
screwdriver
cadere fall
caffè m coffee
caffè ghiacciato
iced coffee
caffè solubile
instant coffee
calce f lime
calcio m kick (n),
football
calcolatrice f
calculator
caldo/a hot, warm

calmo/a calm
calore m heat
calza f stocking
calzini m socks
calzoncini corti
shorts
cambiare change (vb)
cambiavalute bureau
de change
cambio di velocità
gearbox
camera f room
camera con colazione
bed & breakfast
camera d'aria f
inner tube
camera da bagno
bathroom
camera doppia double
room
camera singola
single room
cameriera f maid,
chambermaid
cameriere/a m/f
waiter/waitress
camerino m dressing
room, changing room
camicetta f blouse
camicia f shirt
camicia da notte
nightdress
camino m chimney
camion m truck, lorry
camminare walk (vb)
camminata f walk (n)
camoscio m suede

campagna f
countryside
campanello m bell
**campanello della
  porta** doorbell
campeggiare
camp (vb)
campeggio m
campsite
**campeggio per
  carovane**
caravan site
campo m field
campo da tennis
tennis court
campo di golf golf
course
Canada Canada
canale m canal,
channel
cancellare cancel
cancellazione
cancellation
cancello m gate
cancro m cancer
candela f candle,
spark plug
cane m dog
canna da pesca
fishing rod
canoa f canoe
canotto pneumatico
dinghy
cantante m/f singer
cantare sing
cantina f cellar
canzone f song

capelli m hair
capire understand
capitale f capital (city)
capitale m capital
(money)
capo m head
cappella f chapel
cappello m hat
cappotto m coat,
overcoat
cappuccio m hood
(of garment)
capra f goat
caramella f candy
carbone m coal
carbone di legna m
charcoal
carburante fuel
carburatore m
carburettor
cardigan m cardigan
carello portabagagli
luggage trolley
caricare charge
carino/a pretty
carne f meat
carne di maiale pork
carne di montone
mutton
caro/a dear, expensive
carota f carrot
carovana f caravan
carrello m trolley
**carro attrezzi/
  soccorso**
breakdown van
carrozza f carriage

ITALIAN → ENGLISH

carrozzella f pram
carta f paper
carta assegni cheque
  card
carta avvolgente
  adesiva f cling film
carta d'identità
  identity card
carta d'imbarco
  boarding card
carta da imballaggio
  wrapping paper
carta da lettere f
  writing paper,
  notepaper
carta di credito
  charge card, credit card
carta geografica f
  map
carta stradale f
  road map
cartella f briefcase
cartello stradale m
  road sign
cartoleria f stationer's
cartolina f postcard
cartone m cardboard
casa f house, home
casa colonica
  farmhouse
casco m helmet,
  crash helmet
cassa f till, cash register,
  cash desk
cassetta f cassette
cassetta delle lettere
  post box

cassetta di pronto
  soccorso first-aid kit
cassetto m drawer
cassettone m chest of
  drawers
cassiere/a m/f cashier
castagna f **chestnut**
castello m castle
cattedrale f cathedral
cattivo/a bad, nasty
cattolico/a m/f Catholic
cauto/a careful
cavalcare ride (vb)
cavalcata f ride (n)
cavallo m horse
cavatappi m
  corkscrew
cavi con morsetti
  jump leads
caviglia f ankle
cavolfiore m
  cauliflower
cavolo m cabbage
CE f EC
cena f dinner, supper
centigrado m
  Centigrade
centimetro m
  centimetre
centralinista m/f
  operator (phone)
centrifuga f spin-dryer
centro m centre
centro commerciale
  m shopping centre
centro della città
  city centre

ceppo bloccaruote
wheel clamp

ceramica f pottery

cercare look for

cerchio m circle

cerniera f zipper,
zip fastener

cerotto m sticking
plaster

certamente certainly

certificato m
certificate

certificato di nascita
birth certificate

certo/a certain, sure

cespuglio m bush

cestino m basket

cetriolo m cucumber

champagne m
champagne

Che cosa c'è? What's
the matter

Che cosa non va?
What is wrong?

che lavora in proprio
self-employed

Che ora è? What's the
time?

Chi? Who?

chiamare call (vb)

chiamata f call (n),
telephone call

**chiamata a carico
del destinatario**
reverse-charge call

chiamata di sveglia
wake-up call

chiamata interurbana
long-distance call

chiaro/a clear,
light (adj, not dark)

chiave f key

**chiave dell'
accensione**
ignition key

chiave inglese
spanner

**chiavi per la
macchina** car keys

chiesa f church

chilo m kilo

chilogrammo m
kilogram

chilometro m
kilometre

chiosco m kiosk

chirurgia f surgery
(procedure)

chitarra f guitar

chiudere close, shut,
lock (vb)

chiudere dentro
lock in

chiudere fuori lock out

chiunque anybody

cibo m food

cibo per bambini
baby food

ciclo m cycle

cieco/a blind (adj)

cielo m sky

ciliegia f cherry

cilindro a gas gas
cylinder

ITALIAN → ENGLISH

cima f summit
cimitero m cemetery
Cina f China
cinema m cinema
cinghia f strap
**cinghia del
   ventilatore** fan belt
cinghiale m boar
cintura f belt
cintura di sicurezza f
   seat belt, safety belt
cintura portasoldi
   money belt
cinturino dell'orologio
   watch strap
cioccolato m
   chocolate
cipolla f onion
circa about
   (approximately)
circolo m **del golf**
   golf club (place)
circondato
   surrounded
circonvallazione f
   ring road, bypass
ciste f cyst
cisterna f cistern
cistite f cystitis
città f city, town
cittadino/a m/f citizen
clacson m horn (car)
classe f class
classe economia
   economy class
classificare sort (vb)
clavicola f collar bone

cliente m client,
   customer
clinica f clinic
Coca–cola f Coke
codice m code
codice postale
   postal code
cofano m hood,
   bonnet (of car)
cognac m brandy
cognata f sister-in-law
cognato m
   brother-in-law
cognome m surname
cognome da nubile
   maiden name
coincidenza f
   connection
coito m sex
   (intercourse)
colatoio m colander
colla f glue
collana f necklace
collant m pantyhose,
   tights
collega colleague
colletto m collar
collezionare collect
collo m neck
colluttorio m
   mouthwash
colore m colour
colpo m hit, stroke (n)
coltello m knife
come like (prep)
Come? How?

Come stai?
How are you?
cominciare start
commedia f comedy
commesso m shop
assistant
commissariato m
police station
**commozione
cerebrale**
concussion
comodo/a comfortable,
convenient
compagnia f company
compagno/a m/f
partner (companion)
comperare buy
compilare fill in
compitare spell (vb,
grammar)
compleanno m
birthday
completamente
completely, quite
compositore m
composer
comprare buy
computer m
computer
con with
con giustizia fairly
con speranza
hopefully
concerto m concert
concessione f
concession

condimento m
dressing, seasoning
**condimento per
insalata**
salad dressing
condizione f
condition
condurre lead (vb)
conferenza f
conference
conferma f
confirmation
confermare confirm
confondere confuse,
mix up
congelato frozen
congelatore m
freezer
congestionato
jammed
congiungimento m
junction
congratulazioni
congratulations
coniglio m rabbit
conscio/a conscious
consegna f delivery
consegnare deliver
consolato m
consulate
contatore m meter
contatto m contact (n)
contento/a glad
continuare continue
conto m account, bill
contorno m side dish

ITALIAN → ENGLISH

contraccettivo
contraceptive

contratto m contract

contratto d'affitto m
lease (n)

contro against

controllo m pass
control

controllore m ticket
collector

coperchio m lid

coperta f blanket

coperto m cover
charge

copiare copy

coppia f couple

corda f rope, string

corda del bucato
clothes line

cornice f frame,
picture frame

corno m horn (car)

coro m choir

corona f crown

corpo m body

corrente current (adj)

corrente f current (n)

corrente d'aria
draught

correre run

correttamente
properly

corretto/a correct,
right

corridoio m aisle,
corridor

corriere courier
service

corsa f race (sport)

corse di cavalli
horse racing

corsia f ward (hospital)

corso m course

corso di lingua
language course

corteccia m bark
(n, of tree)

cortese polite

cortile m playground

corto/a short

cosa f thing

Cosa? What?

coscia f thigh

costa f coast

costo m cost

costola f rib

costoletta f chop (n)

costruire build

costume da bagno m
swimming costume

cotone m cotton

cotone idrofilo
cotton wool

cozze fpl mussels

crampo m cramp

cravatta f tie

cravatta a farfalla
bow tie

credere believe

crema idratante
moisturizer

crema pasticciera
custard

crema solare sun
  block
cricco m jack
crimine m crime
cristallo m crystal
crociera f cruise
crollare collapse
crudo/a raw
cuccetta f couchette
cucchiaino (da tè)
  teaspoon
cucchiaio m spoon
cucchiaio (da tavola)
  tablespoon
cucina f kitchen
cucina a gas gas
  cooker
cucinare cook (vb)
cucinino m kitchenette
cucire sew
cuffia fpl earphones
cuffie headphones
cugino m cousin
cuoco m chef, cook (n)
cuore m heart
cupo/a dull
curva f bend
cuscino m cushion
custode m/f caretaker

D
da by (e.g. author), from,
  like (prep)
da qualche parte
  somewhere
da questa parte
  this way

da solo by myself
  (alone)
dado m dice, nut
  (for bolt)
daltonico colour blind
danaroso/a posh
Danimarca f Denmark
danno m damage (n)
dappertutto
  everywhere
dare give
dare fastidio annoy
data di nascita
  date of birth
data di scadenza f
  sell-by date
datteri m dates
davvero really
debiti m debts
debole weak
decaffeinato
  decaffeinated
decidere decide
decisione f decision
decolorante m
  bleach
dedurre deduct
del mattino a.m.
  (before noon)
del pomeriggio p.m.
  (after noon)
deliberatamente
  deliberately
delizioso/a delicious
deluso/a disappointed
denaro contante
  cash

dente m tooth
denti mpl teeth
dentiera dentures
dentista m/f dentist
dentro indoors
dentro a into
depositare deposit (vb)
deposito m deposit (n)
descrivere describe
descrizione
description f
desiderare wish (vb)
desiderio m wish (n)
destro/a right
(direction)
destinazione f
destination
detergente cleaning
solution
**detergente per
trucco** eye make-up
remover
detersivo m washing
powder, detergent
detersivo in polvere
soap powder
detersivo per i piatti
washing-up liquid
deviazione f detour
di of
Di chi? Whose?
di mezzo m middle
di moda fashionable
di nuovo again
di prim'ordine first
class
di qualità upmarket

di seconda
second-hand (used)
di taglia media
medium sized
di valore valuable
diabetico/a m/f
diabetic (adj, n)
diamante m diamond
diarrea f diarrhoea
dicembre m
December
dieta f diet
dietro behind
difetto m fault, flaw
difettoso/a faulty
differenza f difference
difficile difficult
dimenticare forget
dinamo f dynamo
Dio m God
dire say, tell
diretto/a direct
direttore m manager
direzione f direction
diritto/a straight
disastro m disaster
disco m disk
disco parcheggio m
parking disc
disco rigido hard disk
disegno m drawing,
pattern, picture
disfare le valigie
unpack
disinfettante m
disinfectant

disoccupato
unemployed
dispari odd (of
numbers)
disponibile available
disseminare litter (vb)
distanza f distance
**distributore
automatico**
vending machine
disturbare disturb
dito m finger
dito del piede m toe
divano m couch
diverso/a different
divertente funny
divertimento m fun
divertirsi enjoy
dividere share (vb)
divo/a m/f star (film)
divorziato/a divorced
dizionario m
dictionary
doccia f shower
documenti di viaggio
travel documents
documento m
document, record (n)
dogana f customs
dolce sweet (adj)
dolce m dessert,
pudding
dolorante sore
dolore m ache, pain
doloroso/a painful
domanda f enquiry,
question (n)

domandare ask,
question (vb)
domani tomorrow
domani mattina
tomorrow morning
domani pomeriggio
tomorrow afternoon
domani sera
tomorrow evening
domenica f Sunday
domestico/a
domestic
donna f woman
donna poliziotta
policewoman
dopo after
doppio/a double
dormire sleep
dottore m doctor
Dove? Where?
dovere should, must,
owe
dovuto due
dozzina f dozen
dramma m play
(n, theatre)
droga f drug (med)
drogheria f food
shop
due volte twice
durante during
duro/a hard, tough

E
e and
è is

ITALIAN → ENGLISH

È un peccato
It's a pity
ebraico/a Jewish
ebreo m Jew
eccellente excellent
eccetto except
eccitante exciting
economia f economy
edicola f news stand
edificio m building
elastico/a elastic
elenco telefonico m
phonebook
elettricista electrician
elettricità f electricity
elettrico/a electric
elicottero m
helicopter
emergenza f
emergency
emicrania f migraine
entrare come in,
enter
entrata f entrance
entrata forzata
break in
entro le by (time)
epilettico/a m/s
epileptic (adj, n)
equitazione (del
cavallo) horse riding
erano were
erba cipollina chives
erba f grass, herbs
ernia f hernia
errore m error
eruzione f rash

esame m examination
esattamente exactly
esausto/a exhausted
esca f bait
escludere exclude
escursione f
excursion
escursione con
guida guided tour
esecuzione f
performance
esempio m
example
esente da dogana
duty-free
esperto/a
experienced
esplosione f
explosion
esportare export
esposizione f
exposure
espresso/a express
essenziale essential
essere be
essere impaziente di
look forward to
est east
estate f summer
esterno m outside
estintore m fire
extinguisher
Estonia Estonia
estraneo m stranger
età f age
etichetta f label

etichetta per bagagli
  luggage tag
Europa f Europe
europeo/a m/f
  European (adj, n)
evitare avoid

F
fa ago
fa male it's sore
fabbrica f factory
faccenda f matter
faccia f face
facile easy
fagiolo m bean
falegname m
  carpenter
falena f moth
falso/a false, fake
famiglia f family
famoso/a famous
fango m mud
far male hurt
**far pagare più del
  dovuto** overcharged
fare do, make
fare deltaplano m
  hang-gliding
fare il check-in
  check in
fare jogging jog
fare l'autostop
  hitchhike
fare una foto to take
  a photo
farfalla f butterfly
fari mpl headlights

farina f flour
farmacia f pharmacy
farmacista f chemist
fasciatura f dressing
  (bandage)
fatto/a made
fatto a mano
  handmade
fattoria f farm
fattura f invoice
fax fax
fazzolettino di carta
  tissue
fazzoletto m
  handkerchief
febbraio m February
febbre f fever
fede f wedding ring
federa f pillowcase
fegato m liver
felice happy
femmina f female
ferita f injury
ferito/a injured
fermare stop (vb)
**fermare con una
  graffa** staple
fermata f stop (n)
fermata d'autobus
  bus stop
ferro da calza knitting
  needle
ferro da stiro iron
ferrovia f railway
festa f festival, party
  (celebration)

ITALIAN → ENGLISH

festa nazionale public
   holiday
festival m festival
fetta f slice (n)
fiammiferi mpl
   matches (for lighting)
fianco m hip
fiasco m flask
fidanzato/a m/f fiancé,
   fiancée
fidanzato/a engaged
   (to be married)
fiera f fair (fête)
figlia f daughter
figlio m son
fila f queue, row (n)
filetto m fillet
film m film
filo m thread
filo metallico m wire
filtro m filter
filza f file (folder)
finalmente eventually
fine f end (n)
fine settimana
   weekend
finestra f window
finire finish, end (vb)
fino a until, till
fioraio m florist
fiore m flower
firma f signature
firmare sign (vb)
fiume m river
flanella f flannel
fluente fluent
fluido fluent

fodera duvet cover
foglia f leaf
foglia d'alloro
   bay leaf
folla f crowd
fontana f fountain
foratura f puncture
forbici f scissors
forbicine da unghie
   nail scissors
forchetta f fork
foresta f forest
Foresta Nera Black
   Forest
forestiero m
   foreigner
formaggio m cheese
formale formal
formica f ant
fornello m cooker
forno m oven
forno a microonde
   microwave
forse maybe, perhaps
forte loud, strong
fortezza f fortress
fortuna f luck
fortunatamente
   fortunately
fortunato/a lucky
foruncolo m boil
   (n, med)
foschia f mist
**fossa biologica/
   settica f** septic tank
foto f photo

fotocopia f
  photocopy
fragile breakable
fragola f strawberry
frana f landslide
francese French
francese m/f
  Frenchman/woman
Francia f France
francobollo m stamp,
  postage stamp
frase f sentence
  (grammar)
fratello m brother
frattura f fracture
freccia f indicator
freddo/a cold
freno m brake
freno a mano
  handbrake
frequente frequent
fresco/a cool, fresh
fretta quickly
fretta f hurry, rush (n)
friggere fry
frigo m fridge
frittata f omelette
frittella f pancake
fritto fried
frizione f clutch
frizzante fizzy,
  sparkling
frode f rip-off
fronte f forehead
frontiera f border
frutta f fruit
frutti di mare shellfish

fruttivendolo m
  greengrocer
fuga f escape (n)
fumare smoke (vb)
fumo m smoke (n)
funerale m funeral
fungo m mushroom
funicolare f funicular
funivia f cable car
fuochi di Sant'Antonio
  shingles
fuoco m fire
fuori out
fuoristrada f four-
  wheel-drive vehicle
furgone m van
furto m burglary, theft
fusibile m fuse
futuro m future

G
gabbiano m seagull
gabinetto m lavatory,
  toilet
gabinetto medico f
  surgery, doctor's rooms
galleria f gallery,
  tunnel
Galles m Wales
gallese Welsh
gallone m gallon
gamba f leg
gamberetti mpl
  shrimps
gambero m prawn
garage m garage
garanzia f guarantee

ITALIAN → ENGLISH

ITALIAN → ENGLISH

gatto m cat
gelato m ice cream
gelo m frost
geloso/a jealous
gemelli twins
gemelli m cufflinks
generale general (adj)
genero m son-in-law
generoso/a
  generous
genitori m parents
gennaio m January
gente f folk
gentile kind (adj)
genuino/a genuine
gesso m plaster
gettare throw
ghiacciaio m glacier
ghiaccio m ice
ghiaia f shingle
già already
giacca f jacket
giacere lie (vb, recline)
giallo m yellow
giardino m garden
giardino zoologico
  zoo
Ginevra f Geneva
ginocchio m knee
giocare play (vb)
giocattolo m toy
gioco m play (n),
  game
gioia f joy
gioielleria f jeweller's
gioielli m jewellery
giornale m newspaper

giornaliero/a daily
giorno m day
giorno feriale weekday
giostra f roundabout
giovane young
giovedì m Thursday
girare turn
girarsi turn around
giro m tour
giubbotto di
  salvataggio
  life jacket
giudicare judge (vb)
giudice m judge (n)
giugno m June
giuntura f joint
giunzione f junction
giurare swear (an oath)
giusto/a fair, just, right
gli the
goccia f drop (n)
goccie per gli occhi
  eye drops
gola f throat
golf m jumper
gomito m elbow
gomma f rubber, tyre
gomma a terra
  flat tyre
gomma da masticare
  chewing gum
gonfiare swell
gonfio/a swollen
gonfiore m swelling
gonna skirt
gotico/a Gothic
governo government

gradino step
grado m degree (measurement)
gradualment gradually
graffiare scratch (vb)
graffio m scratch (n)
grammatica grammar
grammo gram
Gran Bretagna Great Britain
granaio barn
granchio m crab
grande big, great, large
grande magazzino m department store
grandine f hail
grandioso/a grand
grappolo m bunch (grapes)
grasso/a fat, fatty, greasy
grassoccio/a fatty
grato/a grateful
grattugiare grate
Grecia f Greece
greco m Greek (adj, n)
grembiule m apron
gridare shout (vb)
grido m shout (n)
grigio/a grey
grotta f cave
gruccia f coat hanger
gruppo m group
guaio m trouble
guancia f cheek
guanciale m pillow

guanti m gloves
guardare look at, watch (vb)
guardaroba f cloakroom, wardrobe
guardia f guard
guardia costiera coastguard
guardia di sicurezza security guard
guardiano m caretaker
guasto out of order
guasto m breakdown (car)
guerra f war
gufo m owl
guida f guide (n), tour guide
guida a destra right-hand drive
guida telefonica directory (phone)
guida turistica guide book
guidare drive
gusto m taste (n)

H
hamburger hamburger
handicappato/a handicapped
ho fame I am hungry
Ho voglia di vomitare! I'm going to be sick!
hovercraft m hovercraft

ITALIAN → ENGLISH

161

I
i the
idea f idea
idraulico m plumber
ieri yesterday
ieri notte last night
ieri sera last night
il the
il mio m my
il suo his
il tuo your
il vostro your
illimitato/a unlimited
imitazione f fake (n)
immediatamente
   immediately
immersioni
   subacquee
   scuba diving
immondizia f rubbish,
   refuse (n)
imparare learn
impermeabile
   waterproof (adj)
impermeabile m
   raincoat
impiegato ricezione
   receptionist
importante important
impossibile
   impossible
imposta sul valore
   aggiunto VAT
impostare mail,
   post (vb)
improvvisamente
   suddenly

in in
in buona salute fit,
   healthy
in discesa downhill
in fondo alla at the
   bottom
in modo imparziale
   fairly
in seguito afterwards
in tutto altogether
in un appartamento
   attrezzato di cucina
   self-catering
incantesimo m spell
   (n, magic)
inceppato stuck
inchiostro m ink
incidente m accident,
   road accident
incinta pregnant
incluso included
incontrare meet
incontro m match
   (n, game), meeting
incredibile incredible,
   amazing
incrocio m crossroads
indiano/a m/f Indian
   (adj, n)
indicare point (vb)
indicatore della
   benzina fuel gauge
indigestione f
   indigestion
indipendente
   freelance
infarto heart attack

infenzione f infection
infermiera, infermiere
  nurse, male nurse
infettivo/a infectious
infiammazione f
  inflammation
influenza f flu
informale informal
informazione f
  information
infradito flip flops
ingegnere m engineer
Inghilterra England
inghiottire swallow
inglese English
inglese m/f
  Englishman/woman
ingorgo m traffic jam
ingrandimento m
  enlargement
ingredienti mpl
  ingredients
iniezione f injection
inquinato polluted
insalata f salad
insegnante m/f
  teacher
insegnare teach
insettifugo m
  insect repellent
insetto m insect
insieme together
insistere insist
insolazione f
  sunstroke
insolito/a unusual
insonnia f insomnia

insulina f insulin
intelligente intelligent,
  clever
intelligenza f mind (n)
intendere mean
  (vb, intend)
interdentale
  dental floss
interessante
  interesting
internazionale
  international
interno inside
intero/a whole
interprete m/f
  interpreter
interruttore m switch
interruttore principale
  mains switch
interruzione di
  corrente power cut
intersezione f
  intersection
intervallo m interval
intossicazione
  alimentare food
  poisoning
invalido/a disabled
invece instead
inverno m winter
invertire reverse
investire knock down
invitare invite
invito m invitation
io I
io sono I am
io stesso myself

ITALIAN → ENGLISH

ippodromo m race course

Irlanda f Ireland

Irlanda del Nord f Northern Ireland

irlandese Irish

irlandese m/f Irishman/woman

isola f island

istituto di bellezza beauty salon

Italia f Italy

italiano/a m/f Italian (adj, n)

itterizia f jaundice

L

la the

la f it

là there, over there

l'abbigliamento da donna ladies wear

l'abbigliamento da uomo menswear

l'ufficio postale principale main post office

l'uno o l'altro either of them

la mia f my

laccio m, **laccio da scarpa** shoe lace

ladro/a m/f burglar, thief

lago m lake

Lago di Garda Lake Garda

Lago Maggiore Lake Maggiore

lamentarsi complain

lamentela f complaint

lamette da barba razor blades

lampada f lamp

lampadina f light bulb

lampo m flash, lightning

lampone m raspberry

lana f wool

lancetta dei secondi f second hand (of clock)

largo/a wide

lasciare leave

lasciarsi andare let off (oneself)

lassativo m laxative

lato m side

latta f can (n, tin)

latta per benzina f petrol can

latte m milk

latte in polvere powdered milk

lattina f can (n, tin)

lattuga f lettuce

laurea f degree (qualification)

lavanderia f launderette, laundromat

lavandino m sink, washbasin

lavare wash

lavastoviglie f dishwasher

lavorare work (vb)
lavorare a maglia knit
lavori stradali m
  roadworks
lavoro m job, work (n)
lavoro domestico
  housework
le the
lecca-lecca lollipop
legge f law
leggere read
leggero/a light
  (adj, not heavy)
legno m wood
lei her
lei f she
lentamente slowly
lente f lens
lente d'ingrandimento
  magnifying glass
lenti a contatto
  contact lens
lenticchie f lentils
lento/a slow
lenzuolo m sheet
leone m lion
lepre f hare
lesbica f lesbian
lettera f letter
letti gemelli m
  twin beds
lettino m cot
lettino portatile m
  carry-cot
letto m bed
letto matrimoniale
  double bed

letto singolo single bed
Lettonia f Latvia
lettore di compact
  CD player
leva f lever
leva del cambio gear
  lever
lezione f lesson
libbra f pound (weight)
libero/a free, loose
libreria f bookshop
libretto degli assegni
  cheque book
libro m book (n)
libro di fraseologia
  phrase book
licenza f licence
lieto/a pleased
lima f file (tool)
limetta da unghie f
  nail file
limite di velocità
  speed limit
limonata f lemonade
limone m lemon
lingua f language,
  tongue
lino m linen
liquido per freni brake
  fluid
liquore liqueur
lista f list
lista dei vini wine list
lite f quarrel (n)
litigare quarrel (vb)
litro m litre
Lituania f Lithuania

ITALIAN → ENGLISH

ITALIAN → ENGLISH

livido m bruise (n)
lo the
lo m it
locale local
locanda f inn
lontano/a far
loro they
lotta f fight (n)
lottare fight (vb)
lozione detergente
  cleansing lotion
lucchetto m padlock
luce f light (n)
luce del freno brake
  light
luce del sole
  sunshine
lucidare polish (vb)
lucido m polish (n)
luglio m July
lui he, him
luna f moon
luna di miele
  honeymoon
lunedì m Monday
lungamente long (adv)
lungo/a long (adj)
luogo di villeggiatura
  resort
lupo m wolf
Lussenburgo
  Luxembourg
lusso m luxury

M
ma but
macchia f stain

macchina f car,
  machine
macchina a noleggio
  hire car
macellaio m butcher
madre f mother
magazzino m store,
  warehouse
maggio m May
maggior parte di most
maglia f jersey
maglia (della pelle)
  vest
maglieria f knitwear
maglione m sweater,
  pullover
magnete m magnet
magro low fat
mai never
maiale m pig
maionese f
  mayonnaise
**mal d'auto, d'aereo,
  di nave** travel
  sickness
mal d'orecchi
  earache
mal di denti toothache
mal di gola sore
  throat
mal di mare
  seasickness
mal di schiena
  backache
mal di stomaco
  stomachache
mal di testa headache

malato/a ill
malattia f disease, illness
malattia venerea f venereal disease
malinteso m misunderstanding
mancante missing
mancare miss (vb)
mancia f tip
mancino/a left handed
mandare send
mandarino m tangerine
mandorla f almond
mangiare eat
manifesto m poster
maniglia f handle
mano f hand
manuale manual (adj)
manuale m manual (n)
manzo m beef
marca f brand (n)
marcia f gear
marcia indietro reverse gear
marciapiede m pavement, sidewalk
marcio/a rotten
mare m sea
Mare Baltico Baltic Sea
Mare del Nord m North Sea
marea f tide
marina f navy
marito m husband
marmellata f jam

marmellata d'arance marmalade
marmo m marble (n, stone)
marrone brown
martello m hammer
marzo m March
mascara m mascara
mascella f jaw
maschile male
massa f mass (volume)
materasso m mattress
matita f pencil
matrigna f stepmother
matrimonio m wedding
mattina f morning
mattone m brick
maturo/a ripe
mazza da golf golf club (stick)
mazzo m bunch (of flowers), pack (of cards)
meccanico m mechanic
medicina f medicine
medievale medieval
medio/a medium
mediocre average
mediterraneo Mediterranean
medusa f jellyfish
meglio better
melone m melon

ITALIAN → ENGLISH

ITALIAN → ENGLISH

meningite f
  meningitis
meno less
mensile monthly
menta f mint
mente f mind (n)
mentire lie (vb, fib)
mento m chin
mentre while
menu m menu
menù fisso set menu
menzionare
  mention (vb)
menzione f
  mention (n)
mercato m market
mercoledì m
  Wednesday
meringa f meringue
merluzzo m cod
meschino/a mean
  (adj, nasty)
mescolare mix
mese m month
Messa f mass (rel)
messaggio m
  message
metà f half
metallo m metal
metro m tape measure,
  metre
metropolitana f
  subway, metro
mettere put
mettere in contatto
  contact (vb)
mezzanotte midnight

mezzogiorno m
  midday, noon
mi me
Mi dispiace! Sorry!
Mi fa male It hurts
Mi sento male! I'm
  going to be sick!
miele m honey
miglio m mile
migliorare improve
mille m thousand
minestra f soup
ministro m minister
  (politics)
minuscolo/a tiny
minuto/a minute
  (adj, size)
minuto m minute
  (n, time)
miope short-sighted
mirtilli rossi
  redcurrants
**miscuglio di frutta
  candita** fruit mince
misterioso/a weird
misura f size,
  measure (n)
misurare measure (vb)
mobili mpl furniture
modulo m form
modulo registrazione
  registration form
moglie f wife
molla f spring (metal)
molletta da bucato
  clothes peg
molti many

molto lot
molto/a much, very
Molto lieto!
  How do you do?
Molto piacere!
  Pleased to meet you!
momento m moment
Monaco di Baviera
  Munich
monastero m
  monastery
mondo m world
moneta f coin
montagna f mountain
monumento m
  monument
morbido/a soft
morbillo m measles
mordere bite (vb)
morire die
morso m bite (n)
morte f death
morto/a dead
mosca f fly (n)
moschea f mosque
mostra f exhibition,
  show (n)
mostrare show (vb)
motocicletta f
  motorbike
motore m engine,
  motor
motoscafo m
  motorboat
mucca f cow
multa f fine (n)

**multa per divieto di
  sosta** parking ticket
municipio m town hall
muovere move
muro m wall
muscolo m muscle
museo m museum
musicista m/f
  musician
musulmano m Muslim
mutande f pants,
  underpants
mutandine f knickers,
  panties

N
nafta f diesel
narcotico m drug,
  narcotic
nascita f birth
nascondere hide
naso m nose
nastro m ribbon,
  tape
nastro adesivo m
  adhesive tape
Natale m Christmas
nato/a born
natura f nature
naturale natural
nausea f nausea
nave f boat, ship
navigare sail (vb)
navigazione f sailing
nazionale national
nazionalità f
  nationality

ITALIAN → ENGLISH

ITALIAN → ENGLISH

nè … nè neither … nor

nebbia f fog

necessario/a
necessary

negativo/a negative

negozio m shop

negozio di bricolage
DIY shop

negozio di ferramenta
ironmonger's, hardware
shop

**negozio di
macrobiotica**
health food shop

nel in

neozelandese m/f
New Zealander

nero/a black

nessuno m nobody

neve f snow

nevica It is snowing

nido m nest, crèche

nient'altro nothing
else

niente none, nothing

nipote f niece,
granddaughter

nipote m nephew,
grandson

no no

nocciole f hazelnuts

noce f nut, walnut

noce di cocco
coconut

noi us, we

noioso/a boring

nome m name

nome di battesimo
Christian name,
first name

non not

non fumatori
non-smoking

Non importa
It doesn't matter

non potrei couldn't

non troppo cotto/a
medium rare (meat)

nonna f grandmother

nonni grandparents

nonno m grandfather

nord m north

norvegese m/f
Norwegian

Norvegia f Norway

nostalgia di casa
homesickness

nostro/a our

nota f note

notizie fpl news

notte f night

novembre m
November

nulla nothing

numero m number

numero telefonico m
phone number

nuora f
daughter-in-law

nuotare swim

Nuova Zelanda f
New Zealand

nuovo/a new

nutrire feed (vb)

nuvola f cloud

O

o or
obbligatorio/a compulsory
oca f goose
occhiali m eyeglasses, spectacles, glasses
occhiali da sole sunglasses
occhiali di protezione goggles
occhio m eye
occupato/a busy, engaged, occupied
occupazione f occupation
oceano m ocean
odorare smell (vb)
odore m smell (n)
oggetti smarriti lost property
oggi m today
ogni each, every
ogni ora hourly
ogni tanto occasionally
ognuno everyone
olandese Dutch
oleoso/a greasy
olio m oil
olio di oliva olive oil
olio solare suntan oil
oliva f olive
oltre beyond
ombra f shade
ombrello m umbrella
ombretto m eye shadow

omelette f omelette
omosessuale gay
onda f wave
onesto/a honest
opera f opera
operatore turistico m tour operator
operazione f operation
opposto/a opposite
opuscolo m brochure
ora f hour, time
orario m timetable
orario d'apertura opening times
orario delle visite visiting hours
orchestra f orchestra
ordinare order (vb)
ordine m order (n)
orecchini earrings
orecchio m ear
orecchioni mpl mumps
organico/a organic (vegetables)
orlo m hem
ormeggio m mooring
oro m gold
orologio m clock, watch (n)
ospedale m hospital
ospitalità f hospitality
ospitare put up (guest)
ospite m/f visitor, guest
osso m bone
ostello m hostel
ostello della gioventù youth hostel

ITALIAN → ENGLISH

ottenere obtain
ottico m optician
ottobre m October
ovest m west

P
pacchetto m packet
pacco m package,
  parcel
pacemaker m
  pacemaker
padella f pan,
  frying pan
padiglione m ward
  (hospital)
padre m father
paese m country
Paesi Bassi
  Netherlands
pagamento m
  payment
pagare pay
pagato paid
pagina f page
pagine gialle
  Yellow Pages
paglia f straw
pagnotta f loaf
paio m pair
palazzo m palace
palestra f gym
paletta per la
  spazzatura
  dustpan
pallido/a pale
pallina f marble (n, toy)
palude f marsh

pancetta f bacon
panciotto m waistcoat
pane m bread
pane di segale f rye
  bread
pane integrale
  wholemeal bread
panfilo m yacht
panificio m bakery
panino m roll
panna f cream,
  breakdown (of car)
panna montata f
  whipped cream
pannolini usa e getta
  disposable diapers/
  nappies
pannolino m diaper,
  nappy
pantaloni m trousers
pantofole f slippers
papavero m poppy
parabrezza
  windscreen
parafango m fender
parasole m sunshade
paraurti m bumper
  (car)
parcheggiare park (vb)
parchimetro m
  parking meter
parco m park (n)
parecchi several
parente m/f
  relative, relation
parenti acquisiti m
  in-laws

parlare speak, talk
parola f word
parolaccia f swear
  word
parole crociate
  crossword puzzle
parrucca f wig
parrucchiere/a m/f
  hairdresser
parte f part, share (n)
partenza f departure
particolari m details
particolarmente
  especially
partire depart
partita di calcio
  football match
partito m party
  (political)
Pasqua Easter
passaggio a livello
  level crossing
passaggio pedonale
  crossing, pedestrian
  crossing
passaporto m
  passport
passare pass (vb)
passato/a past
passeggero m
  passenger
passeggiata f walk (n)
passeggino m baby
  buggy, pushchair
passo m pass (n)
pasta f pastry

pasticceria f
  cake shop
pastiglie per la gola
  throat lozenges
pasto m meal
pastore m minister
  (church)
patata f potato
patatine fritte chips,
  crisps, French fries
patente f licence
patente di guida
  driving licence
patrigno m
  stepfather
pattinare skate (vb)
pattini da ghiaccio
  ice skates
pattino m skate (n)
patto m deal
pattumiera f dustbin,
  bin, waste bin
paura, paura di
  afraid, afraid of
pavimento m floor
paziente patient (adj)
paziente m/f
  patient (n)
pazzo/a mad
peccato pity
pecora f sheep
pedaggio toll
pedale m pedal
pedone m pedestrian
peggio/a worse
pelle f leather, skin
pelliccia f fur coat

ITALIAN → ENGLISH

pellicola f film
pelo m fur
penisola f peninsula
penna f pen
penna a sfera
ballpoint pen
pensare think
pensionato m
old-age pensioner
pensione f boarding
house, guesthouse
pensione completa
full board
pepe m pepper
per for, per
per esempio for
example
per favore please
per la notte overnight
per lo più mostly
pera f pear
Perchè Why?
perchè because
percorso m way
perdere lose, leak (vb)
perdita f leak (n)
perduto/a lost
perfetto/a perfect
pericolo m danger
pericoloso/a
dangerous
periodo m period
perla f pearl
permanente perm
permesso permit (n)
permesso di pesca
fishing permit

permesso per caccia
hunting permit
permettere allow, let,
permit (vb)
pernottare stop over
persona f person
persone f people
pesante heavy
pesare weigh
pesca f peach
pesce m fish
pescivendolo m
fishmonger's
peso m weight
pettine m comb
petto m chest
pezzi di ricambio
car parts
pezzo m bit, piece
pezzo di ricambio
spare part
piacere like (vb)
piangere cry
piano m piano, storey
pianta f plant (n),
sole (foot)
pianta stradale
street map
piantare plant (vb)
pianterreno m
ground floor
piattino m saucer
piatto m dish, plate
piatto da asporto/
piatto da portar via
take-away food
piazza f square (n)

picco m   peak
piccolo/a   small, little
picnic m   picnic
piede m   foot
piedi mpl   feet
pieno/a   full
pietra f   stone
pigiama f   pyjamas
pigro/a   lazy
pila f   flashlight
pillola f   pill
pilota f   pilot
pinne f   flippers
pinze f   pliers
pinzette f   tweezers
pioggia f   rain
piolo m   peg
piolo da tenda   tent
  peg
piombatura   filling
  (tooth)
piombo m   lead (n)
pipa f   pipe
**pirofilo/resistente al
  calore**   ovenproof
pirosi   heartburn
**piscina coperta/
  interna**   indoor pool
pisello m   pea
pista di pattinaggio
  ice rink, skating rink
pista per biciclette
  cycle track
pista per principianti
  nursery slope
pista per sci   ski slope
pistola f   gun

pittura f   paint (n)
pitturare   paint (vb)
piu   extra
più   more
più tardi   later
piumone m   duvet
pizzo m   lace (fabric)
plastica f   plastic
pochi   few
poco/a   little
poco profondo
  shallow
polacco m   Polish
polizia f   police
poliziotto m
  policeman
pollice m   inch, thumb
pollo m   chicken
polmone m   lung
Polonia f   Poland
polso m   wrist
poltrona f   armchair
polvere f   dust,
  powder
pomata f   ointment
pomeriggio m
  afternoon
pomodoro m
  tomato
pompa f   pump (n)
pompare   pump (vb)
ponte m   bridge
popolare   popular
popolazione
  population
porcellana f   china
porre   place (vb)

ITALIAN → ENGLISH

porro m   leek
porta f   door
portabagagli m
   roof-rack, luggage rack,
   boot (car)
portachiavi m   key ring
portafoglio m   wallet
portare   bring, carry,
   wear
portata principale
   main course
portiere m   doorman,
   porter
portinaio/a m/f   janitor
porto m   port, harbour
Portogallo m   Portugal
portoghese m/f
   Portuguese
porzione f   portion
posare   place (vb)
posate   cutlery
possibile   possible
posta f   post, mail (n)
posta aerea f   airmail
posta raccomandata
   registered mail
posteggio per taxi
   taxi rank
postino/a m/f
   postman/woman
posto m   place (n)
posto al finestrino
   window seat
posto sul corridoio
   aisle seat
posto vacante
   vacancy

**postumi di una
   sbornia**   hangover
potere   can (vb, be able
   to), may, might
potrei   could
povero/a   poor
   (impoverished)
pozza f   pool
pranzo m   lunch
pratica f   practice
praticare   practise
preciso/a   accurate
preferire   prefer
preferito/a   favourite
prefisso m   dialling
   code
pregare   pray
premio m   prize
prendere   take, catch
prendere a calci
   kick (vb)
prendere a prestito
   borrow
**prendere un biglietto
   per**   book (vb, ticket)
prenotazione f
   reservation (seats)
preoccupato/a
   worried
presa di corrente
   socket
presentare   introduce,
   present (vb)
presente   present (adj)
preservativo m
   condom
pressappoco   roughly

pressione f pressure
**pressione alta
  del sangue**
  high blood pressure
pressione del sangue
  blood pressure
**pressione delle
  gomme**
  tyre pressure
prestare lend
presto soon, quickly
prete m priest
previsioni del tempo
  weather forecast
prezzo m price
prigione f prison
prima classe first class
prima colazione
  breakfast
prima di before
primavera f spring
  (season)
primo/a first
Primo Ministro m
  prime minister
primo piano first floor
principale main
principiante beginner
privato/a private
privo di sensi
  unconscious
probabilmente
  probably
problema m problem
profondo/a deep
profumo m perfume

programma m
  programme, program
proibito forbidden
prolunga extension
  lead
prolungamento m
  extension
promessa f promise
pronto ready
pronto soccorso m
  casualty department,
  first aid
pronunciare
  pronounce
proprietaria f
  landlady
proprietario m
  landlord, owner
proprio just (only)
prosciutto m ham
prossima settimana
  next week
prossimo/a next
protestante
  Protestant
provare try
provarsi try on
prugna f plum
prurito m itch (n)
pubblicità f advert,
  advertisement
pubblico/a public
pubblico m audience
pulce f flea
pulito/a clean
pungere sting (vb)
puntine f points (car)

ITALIAN → ENGLISH

punto m point (n),
  stitch
puntura f sting (n)
puntura di insetto m
  insect bite
purè di patate
  mashed potatoes

Q

qua here
quadrante m dial (n)
quadrato/a square
  (adj, shape)
quadro m painting
  (picture)
qualche some
qualche cosa
  anything
qualche volta
  sometimes
qualcosa something,
  anything
qualcuno m
  someone, somebody
Quale? Which?
qualità f quality
Quando? When?
Quanti? How many?
quantità f amount,
  quantity
**Quanto costa
  questo?**
  How much is it?
Quanto le devo? How
  much do I owe you?
quarantena f
  quarantine

quarto m quarter
quasi almost, nearly
quegli m those
quei those
quel that
quelli those
quello that
quercia f oak
questa sera f tonight
questa settimana
  this week
questo/a this
qui here, over here
quindicina f fortnight
quota d'entrata
  admission fee,
  entrance fee

R

rabbia f rabies
racchetta f racket
racchetta da tennis
  tennis racket
raccolta f harvest
raccomandare
  recommend
raccordo m junction
radere shave
radiatore m radiator
radio f radio
raffreddore da fieno
  hay fever
ragazza f girl,
  girlfriend
ragazzo m boy,
  boyfriend
raggi-X m X-ray

raggio m spoke
ragionevole
  reasonable
ragnatela f web
ragno m spider
rana f frog
rapportare report (vb)
rapporto m report (n)
rappresentante m
  sales representative
raro/a rare
rasoio m razor
rastrello m rake
rattura f tear (n)
ravanello m radish
razza f race (people)
re m king
reale royal
realizzare realize
recentemente
  recently
recinto m fence
regalo m gift, present
regalo di nozze
  wedding present
regalo per il
  compleanno
  birthday present
reggiseno m bra
regina f queen
regione f district,
  region
registrare register,
  record (vb)
registratore m
  tape recorder
registro m register (n)

Regno Unito m U.K.
regolo m ruler (for
  measuring)
remare row (vb)
remo m oar
rene m kidney
Repubblica Ceca
  Czech Republic
residente m/f resident
respirare breathe
respiratore m snorkel
restare remain
restituire give back
resto m rest (n,
  remainder)
restringersi shrink
rete f net
reumatismo m
  rheumatism
riagganciare
  hang up (phone)
ribes neri
  blackcurrants
ricaricare recharge
riccio/a curly
ricco/a rich
ricetta f prescription,
  recipe
ricevere get
ricevitore m receiver
ricevuta f receipt
ricezione f reception
richiedere require,
  request (vb)
richiesta f request (n)
riconoscere
  recognize

ricordare remember
ricordo souvenir m
  souvenir
ridere laugh (vb)
ridicolo/a ridiculous
ridurre reduce
riduzione f reduction
riempire fill
riempirsi fill up
rifiutare refuse (vb)
rifiuti mpl litter (n)
rimandare postpone
rimanere stay
rimborsare refund (vb)
rimborso m refund (n)
rimorchiare tow
rimorchio m trailer
ringraziare thank
riparare mend,
  repair (vb)
riparazione f repair (n)
ripetere repeat
ripido/a steep
ripieno m stuffed
riposare rest (vb)
riposo rest (n,
  relaxation)
risata f laugh (n)
riscaldamento
  heating
**riscaldamento
  centrale**
  central heating
riserva f reserve
riserva naturale f
  nature reserve
riso m rice

rispondere answer,
  reply (vb)
risposta f answer,
  reply (n)
ritardare delay (vb)
ritardo/a late
ritardo m delay (n)
ritirato/a sheltered
ritiro bagagli
  baggage reclaim
ritornare return (vb),
  come back, go back
ritorno m return (n)
ritratto m portrait
riva f shore
rivista f magazine
rivoltante revolting
roccia f rock
romanzo m novel
rompere break,
  tear (vb)
rosa pink
rosa f rose
rosolia f German
  measles, rubella
rossetto m lipstick
rosso red
rosso per le guancie
  blusher
rotolo m coil
rotondo/a round
rotto/a broken
rovesciare knock over,
  spill
rovina f ruin (n)
rovinare ruin (vb), spoil
rubare steal

ITALIAN → ENGLISH

rubato stolen
rughe f wrinkles
rullino a colori
  colour film
rum m rum
rumore m noise,
  row (n)
rumoroso/a noisy
ruota f wheel
ruota di scorta
  spare tyre/wheel
ruscello m stream
russare snore
ruvido/a rough

S
sabato Saturday
sabbia f sand
sacchetto di plastica
  plastic bag
sacco a pelo m
  sleeping bag
sala f hall
sala d'aspetto
  waiting room
sala da pranzo
  dining room
sala delle partenze
  departure lounge
sala di prova f
  fitting room
salario m wage
salato/a savoury
sale m salt
salire get on, climb
salmone m salmon
salmone affumicato
  smoked salmon

salotto m lounge
salsa f sauce
salsiccia f sausage
saltare jump
Salute! cheers!
saluto m greeting
salvagente m life belt
salvamento m
  rescue (n)
salvare rescue (vb),
  save
sandali mpl sandals
sangue m blood
sanguinare bleed
sano/a healthy
santo/a holy
sapere know
sapone m soap
sapore m flavour
saporito savoury
sarto m tailor
sbagliato/a wrong
sbaglio m mistake
sbucciare peel (vb)
scacchi m chess
scadente cheap
scadere expire
scaffale m shelf
scala f ladder
scala mobile
  escalator
scalare climb
scale f stairs
scambiare exchange
scandente poor
  (quality)
scarafaggio m
  cockroach

scarpa f shoe
scarponi da sci
  ski boot
scarto m waste (n)
scatola f box, can
scatola dei fusibili
  fuse box
scatola di cartone
  carton
scegliere choose
scenario m scenery
scendere get off
scheda telefonica f
  phone card
scheggia f splinter
schermo m screen
scherzo m joke
schiantare crash (vb)
schiena f back
sci m ski (n)
sci acquatico
  waterskiing
sciare ski (vb)
sciarpa f scarf
sciocco/a silly
sciogliere melt
sciopero m strike
sciroppo per la tosse
  cough mixture
scivolare slide, slip (vb)
scivolata f slip (n)
scivolo m slide (n)
scivoloso slippery
scodella f bowl
scogliera f cliff
scola pasta f
  colander

scommessa bet (n)
scommettere bet (vb)
scomodo/a
  inconvenient,
  uncomfortable
scomparire disappear
scompartimento m
  compartment
sconto m discount
sconto per studenti
  student discount
scopa f broom
scoppiare burst
scoprire discover
scorciatoia f short-cut
scorrevole fluent
scorsa settimana
  last week
scorta f stock
scottatura f sunburn
Scozia f Scotland
scozzese m/f Scot,
  Scottish (n, adj)
scrivere write
scuola f school
scuola materna f
  nursery school
scuotere shake
scuro/a dark
scusa f apology
scusi excuse me
Scusi? Pardon?
sdraiarsi lie down
se if
sebbene although
secchio m bucket,
  pail

secolo m century
seconda classe
  second class
secondo/a second
  (adj, number)
secondo m second
  (n, of time)
sedano m celery
sedere sit
sedia f chair, seat
sedia a rotelle
  wheelchair
sedia a sdraio
  deck chair
seggiolino per
  macchina
  child car seat
seggiolone m
  high chair
seggiovia f chair lift
segnale stradale f
  signpost
segnale m signal
segnale di linea libera
  dialling tone
segnale stradale
  road sign
segno m sign (n)
segretario m
  secretary
seguire follow
self service self-
  service
sella f saddle
semaforo m traffic
  light

seminterrato m
  basement
semplice plain, simple
sempre always
senape f mustard
seno m breast
senso unico
  one-way street
sentenza f sentence
  (law)
sentiero m lane, path,
  footpath
sentire feel, hear
senza without
senza reggiseno
  topless
senza zucchero
  sugar-free
separare
  separate (vb)
separato/a
  separate (adj)
sera f evening
serbatoio m tank
serio/a serious
serpente m snake
serranda f shutter
serratura f lock (n)
serratura automatica
  central locking
servizio m service,
  service charge
sesso m sex (gender)
seta f silk
setaccio m sieve
settembre m
  September

ITALIAN → ENGLISH

settico/a septic
settimana week
settimanale weekly
sezione department
sfuggire escape (vb)
shampoo e messa in piega
  shampoo and set
si yes
sicuramente definitely
sicuro/a sure, safe
sidro m cider
sigaretta f cigarette
sigaro m cigar
Signor m Mr
signora f lady
Signora f, **signorina** f
  Mrs/Ms
signorina Miss
silenzio m silence
simile similar, like (adj)
sinagoga f
  synagogue
sinistra left
sistemare arrange
slitta f sledge
slogare sprain (vb)
smalto per unghie m
  nail varnish/polish
sobborgo m suburb
sobrio/a sober
soccorso alpino
  mountain rescue
socio m partner
  (business)
soda f soda
soffitta f attic

soffitto m ceiling
soggiorno m
  living room
sogliola f sole (fish)
soldi m money
sole m sun
sollevare lift (vb)
solo alone, only,
  single
solubile soluble
soluzione per lenti a contatto soaking
  solution
sonnifero m
  sleeping pill
sono are, am
sopra above, over, on
sordo/a deaf
sorella f sister
sorgente calda hot
  spring
sorpassare overtake
sorridere smile (vb)
sorriso m smile (n)
sorta f kind (n)
sospensione f
  suspension
sostituto di fianco
  hip replacement
sottile thin
sotto below, under
sottosopra
  upside down
sottoterra
  underground
sottotitolo m subtitle

sovrano m ruler (sovereign)
Spagna f Spain
spagnoli/e m/f Spanish
spagnolo/a m/f Spaniard
spalla f shoulder
spazzatura f trash
spazzola f brush
spazzola per capelli hairbrush
spazzolino da denti toothbrush
spazzolino da unghie m nail brush
spazzolino per le unghie scrubbing brush
specchietto retrovisore rear-view mirror
specchio m mirror
specialità speciality
specie f sort (n)
spegnere turn off, switch off
spendere spend
spento off
speranza f hope (n)
sperare hope (vb)
spese fpl expenses
spesso often
spesso/a thick
spettacolo burattini m puppet show
spezia f spice

spiaggia f beach, seaside
spiaggia per nudisti nudist beach
spiccioli mpl change (n, coins)
spiegare explain
spilla f brooch
spillo m pin
spillo di sicurezza m safety pin
spina f plug (elec), thorn
spina dorsale f spine
spinaci m spinach
spingere push
spirito m spirits
splendere shine
spogliatoio m changing room (for sports)
sporco/a dirty
sportello automatico auto-teller, cash dispenser
sposa f bride
sposato/a married
sposo m bridegroom
sprecare waste (vb)
spugna f sponge
spuntato/a blunt
spuntino m snack
squadra f team
staccato/a disconnected
stadio m stadium
stagione f season
stagnola f tinfoil

ITALIAN → ENGLISH

ITALIAN → ENGLISH

stamattina this morning
stampa f print (n)
stampare print (vb)
stampe printed matter
stampella f coat hanger
stampelle f crutches
stanco/a tired
stantio/a stale
stanza ammobiliata furnished
stanza dei bambini nursery
starnutire sneeze (vb)
starnuto m sneeze (n)
stasera tonight
Stati Uniti (d'America) United States
statua f statue
stazione f station
stazione di servizio petrol station
stazione ferroviaria railway station
stazione termale f spa
stella f star (sky)
sterlina f pound (money)
sterzare steer
stesso/a same
stitico/a constipated
stivale m boot (shoe)
stivali boots
stoffa f material
stomaco m stomach

stomatite mouth ulcer
storia f history
storico/a historic
stoviglie f crockery
straccio m rag
straccio per pavimento floorcloth
stracotto overdone
strada f road, street
strada a pedaggio toll road
strada principale main road
straniero/a foreign
straniero m foreigner
strano/a odd, peculiar, strange
straordinario/a extraordinary
strato di ghiaccio invisibile black ice
stretto/a narrow, tight
strofinaccio m dishtowel, duster
studente m student
stufa heater
stufato m stew
stupefacente astonishing
stupido/a stupid
stuzzicadente toothpick
su on, up
subito straightaway
succedere happen
succhiotto m dummy

succo m juice
succo d'arancia
  orange juice
succo di frutta
  fruit juice
succo di pomodoro
  tomato juice
succursale f branch
  (office)
sud m south
Sudafrica f South
  Africa
sudafricano/a m/f
  South African (adj, n)
sudare sweat (vb)
sudicio/a filthy
sudore m sweat (n)
sugo di carne gravy
suocera f
  mother-in-law
suoceri m
  parents-in-law
suocero m
  father-in-law
suola f sole (shoe)
suolo m ground
suonare ring (vb)
supplemento m
  supplement
surriscaldare
  overheat
svedese m/f Swede,
  Swedish (n, adj)
svegliarsi wake up
sveglio awake
svenire faint (vb)
Svezia f Sweden

sviluppare develop,
  film processing
svitare unscrew
Svizzera f Switzerland
svizzero/a m/f Swiss
svizzero/a tedesco/a
  m/f Swiss-German

T
tabellone noticeboard
tacchino m turkey
tacco m heel (shoe)
taccuino m notebook
tachimetro m
  speedometer
tagliare (a pezzi)
  chop, cut (vb)
tagliente sharp
taglio m cut (n)
taglio di capelli
  haircut
talco m talcum powder
tallone m heel (foot)
tampone m tampon
tappeto m carpet, rug
tappo m cork, top,
  plug (bath)
tardi late
targa f number plate,
  registration number
tariffa f fare
tariffa economica
  cheap rate
tariffa massima f
  peak rate
tasca f pocket
tassa f tax

ITALIAN → ENGLISH

tassì m   cab, taxi
tassista m/f   taxi
driver
tasso m   rate
(of exchange)
tavola da surf
surfboard
tavoletta di cioccolato
bar of chocolate
tavolo m   table
taxi m   cab, taxi
tazza f   cup
tè   tea
teatro m   theatre
tedesco/a m/f
German (adj, n)
teiera f   teapot
telefonare a carico
del destinatario
collect call
telefonata f   phone call
telefono m   phone,
telephone
telefono cellulare
mobile phone
telefono pubblico m
payphone
televisione f   television
temperatura f
temperature
tempesta f   storm
tempia f   temple (anat)
tempio m   temple (rel)
tempo m   weather
temporale m
thunderstorm

temporaneo/a
temporary
tenda f   curtain, tent
tenda veneziana f
blind (n, for window)
tendine m   tendon
tenere   keep, hold
Tenga il resto!
Keep the change!
tennis m   tennis
tergicristallo m
windscreen wiper
terminale   terminal
termometro m
thermometer
termosifone   heater
terra f   earth, land,
ground
terremoto m
earthquake
terribile   dreadful
tessuto m   cloth
tessuto sintetico
man-made fibre
testa f   head
testimone m/f
witness
tettarella f   teat
tetto m   roof
tettuccio apribile
sunroof
timido/a   shy
timone m   rudder
tintoria   dry cleaner's
tintura f   dye
tipico/a   typical
tipo m   type

tirare pull
tirare diritto
  straight on
tisana f herbal tea
toilette toilet
toilette per donne
  ladies' toilet
toilette per uomini
  gents' toilet
tonno m tuna
tonsillite f tonsillitis
topo m mouse, rat
torcia f torch
torre f tower
torta f cake, pie
tosse f cough (n)
tossire cough (vb)
totale m total
tovaglia f tablecloth
tovaglioli di carta
  paper napkins
tovagliolo m napkin
tra among
tradurre translate
traduttore m
  translator
traduzione f
  translation
traffico m traffic
traghetto m ferry,
  car ferry
tram m tram
tramezzino m
  sandwich
tramonto m sunset
trampolino m
  diving board

trampolino per sci
  ski jump
tranquillante m
  tranquillizer
tranquillo/a quiet
trapano m drill (n)
trapunta f quilt
treccia f plait
treno m train
triste sad
tromba f horn (car)
trota f trout
trovare find
tu you
tubo di scappamento
  m exhaust pipe
tubo di scarico drain
tubo flessibile
  hose pipe
tuffarsi dive (vb)
tuono m thunder
tuorlo m yolk
turchese turquoise
Turchia f Turkey
turco/a m/f Turk,
  Turkish (n, adj)
tuta da ginnastica f
  tracksuit
tutti e due both
tutto everything
tutto/a whole

U
ubriaco/a drunk
uccello m bird
uccidere kill
UE f EU

ITALIAN → ENGLISH

ufficio m office
ufficio informazioni
  enquiry desk
ufficio postale
  post office
uguale even
ulcera f ulcer
ulteriore further
ultimo/a last
ultimo piano top
  floor
umido/a damp,
  humid
umorismo m
  humour
un altro another
una scatola di
  cioccolatini
  chocolates (box of)
una settimana fa
  a week ago
una volta f once
ungherese m/f
  Hungarian (adj, n)
Ungheria f Hungary
unghia f nail
unire join
università university
uno, una one
untuoso/a greasy
uomini m men
uomo m man
uova strapazzate
  scrambled eggs
uovo m egg
uovo di Pasqua
  Easter egg

uovo in camicia
  poached egg
urgente urgent
usanza f custom
usare use
usato second-hand,
  used
uscita f exit
uscita di sicurezza
  emergency exit,
  fire exit
usuale, di solito
  usual, usually
utensili da cucina
  cooking utensils
utile useful
uva grape
uva passa raisin

V
va bene all right, okay
vacanza f holiday,
  vacation
vacanza organizzata
  package holiday
vacanze holidays
vaccinazione f
  vaccination
vaglia postale
  money order
vagone m coach
  (railway)
vagone letto
  sleeping car
vagone ristorante
  buffet car
valanga f avalanche
valido/a valid

valigia f case, suitcase
valle f valley
valore m worth,
  value (n)
valuta f currency
valutare value (vb)
valvola f valve
vanga f spade
vaniglia f vanilla
vapore m steam
varicella f chicken pox
vassoio m tray
vecchio/a old
vedere see
vedova f **vedovo** m
  widow, widower
vegetariano m
  vegetarian
veicolo m vehicle
**veicolo a trazione a
  4 ruote** four-wheel-
  drive vehicle
vela f sail (n)
veleno m poison
velenoso/a poisonous
veloce fast
velocità f speed
vena f vein
vendere sell
vendita f sale
venditore m
  salesperson
venerdì Friday
Venerdì Santo
  Good Friday
venire come
venire a prendere
  fetch

ventilatore m fan
vento m wind
ventoso/a windy
verde green
verdure f vegetables
vergogna f shame
verificare check (vb)
verme m maggot
vero/a real, true
versare pour
vertiginoso/a dizzy
vescica f blister
vespa f wasp
vestaglia f dressing
  gown
vestiti m clothes
vestito m dress, suit
veterinario m vet
  (veterinarian)
vetrina f shop window
via via, by, away
viaggiare travel
viaggio m journey
viaggio d'affari
  business trip
viaggio in nave
  boat trip
viale m avenue
vicino/a m/f neighbour
vicino near, nearby
Vienna f Vienna
vietato prohibited
vigili del fuoco
  fire brigade
Vigilia di Capodanno
  New Year's Eve
Vigilia di Natale
  Christmas Eve

ITALIAN → ENGLISH

ITALIAN → ENGLISH

vigneto m vineyard
villaggio m village
vincere win
vino m wine
vino amabile medium dry (wine)
vino da tavola table wine
vino di casa house wine
Vino di Oporto m port (wine)
vino rosso m red wine
viola purple
violazione f rape (n)
violentare rape (vb)
violetto f violet
virus m virus
visita f visit (n)
visitare visit (vb)
vista f sight, view
visto m visa
vita f life, waist
vite f screw (n)
vitello m veal, calf
vivace lively
vivere live
voce f voice
voi you
volante steering wheel
volantino m leaflet
volare fly (vb)
volere want
volo m flight
volo charter charter flight

volo coincidenza connecting flight
volpe f fox
voltaggio m voltage
vomitare vomit
vulcano m volcano
vuoto/a empty

Z
zaino m backpack
zanzara f mosquito
zero m zero
zia f aunt
zio m uncle
zona f zone
zoo m zoo
zucchero m sugar